FAITH AT WORK

A short history of the birth and

early life of OASIS

Graham Mungeam

Published by Oasis

ISBN-13: 978-0-9554128-0-6
ISBN-10: 0-9554128-0-3

Oasis
1a Kennington Road
London
SE1 7QP

FAITH AT WORK
Contents

Dedication

This book is dedicated to the memory of Daniel Banerjee of Oasis India, who died just as the final chapter was being written, and others who have died in recent years - Pastor George of Oasis Uganda, Dave McGavin, Pete McCahon and Bronwyn Mulcahy of Oasis UK, and Penny Relph who served Oasis and Christmas Cracker. All these friends and colleagues died in the prime of their lives. They were much loved and valued members of the Oasis family and we thank God for them all.

Acknowledgements

I would like to thank the many members of Oasis, past and present who have helped in the writing of this book, and all those whom I have consulted on its accuracy.

Special thanks go to Joan Carter-Smith for the many hours she has spent typing and correcting the manuscript; to Lyn Ransom who supported me in many ways in the UK office, and read through the final draft; to Julia Honey and Roger and Sue Wates who also read the document and made helpful suggestions; and to Margaret Lock who edited the text. I am grateful to Steve Chalke and Andy Matheson who provided time to talk through issues and clarify my memory. Needless to say, I take full responsibility for the final product. If there are any serious errors, please let me know.

Finally, I would like to thank my wife, Margaret, for her patience and support during the writing of this book.

Graham Mungeam
Tonbridge
July 2006

Preface

This short history is written as an *aide memoire* for those who were associated with and witnessed the birth of Oasis in 1985; those who were directly involved in its early days; and the many (mainly young) people who devoted a part of their lives to building up its life and witness over the years and without whose commitment and enthusiasm there would have been no story to tell. Oasis owes them all a debt of gratitude. I hope the book will also be a help and inspiration for all those who will follow them, whether as members of staff or as volunteers throughout the world.

Last but not least, it is written to thank the many people who have supported and stood by Oasis through its ups and downs over the years, and to whom, under God, Oasis is accountable.

Above all, I hope that the account will be read as a witness to the faithfulness of God without whose love, forgiveness, forbearance, guidance and inspiration, the story would not have been possible.

The book is written by an 'insider' with all the strengths and weaknesses which that entails. Other people may, perhaps, have different views and perspectives, but I have sought to verify its accuracy as far as possible with all the principal actors.

'Faith at Work' is not a history which is told sequentially from the beginning to the end. Instead the various chapters address subjects and themes that may overlap in time. It is, therefore, suitable for selective reading according to the interests of each reader.

There is a significant break between the first six chapters, which are concerned exclusively with Oasis in the UK, and chapters eight and nine, dealing with the start of work in other countries. This is bridged by chapter seven on 'Christmas Cracker', which was run in partnership with other organisations as a separate charity. Although there are short passages on the origins and early development of Oasis work in locations outside the UK, each has its own story to tell which could provide material for many more books in the future!

The book is not principally about administration, management or finance. Readers who are interested in these matters, especially as they apply to newly formed charities, may wish to refer to chapters eleven to thirteen inclusive.

Finally, the book speaks a great deal about policies, plans, activities, projects, programmes and structures. It explains the visions and ideas that gave rise to the projects and refers to the people who ran them. Underneath all these, however, is the commitment to Christ of numerous individuals and organisations; the prayers of Oasis supporters throughout the world; and the shared belief of all those who see Christ and His gospel as the only hope of a troubled world.

Chapter 14 looks to the future. It is only as Christians live out their faith in ways that are pleasing to God that the transformation in individual lives and in society, to which Oasis is committed, can be brought about.

Chapter 1
Genesis

"If the story of Jesus is true then I must spend my life telling people about it." With this compelling logic Steve Chalke committed his life to the service of Christ. He had become a Christian following a youth event, run by students of Spurgeon's College, at Holmesdale Road Baptist Church, south London. As a 14 year old he had been challenged by his youth leader to take the Gospel seriously and not simply to go along with the many young people in his group who heard the message week by week but for whom it had little material or lasting significance. Having made his commitment, Steve was then consumed by a vision - to set up a hostel for the homeless, a school and a hospital.

Born in November 1955, the eldest of three children, Steve had attended church throughout his life. The son of an Indian father and an English mother, he had been taught about Jesus from his earliest days. But life had otherwise been far from easy. Growing up as a boy he had observed society's treatment of his father who had arrived in England from Madras in the early '50s. Victor Chalke was a well educated man but, like so many immigrants to Britain before and since, he had had great difficulty finding suitable employment, eventually accepting a job as a cleaner in the canteen of a London Transport bus depot. Later he worked for many years as a porter on British Rail, another job well below his ability and potential.

All this made a deep impression on the young Chalke who, because his skin was darker than that of his fellow pupils, was himself experiencing some racial prejudice and abuse. He was also becoming aware of the needs of other poor and marginalised groups in society, and at the age of 13 regularly visited homeless people, or 'tramps' as they were known, under the arches of Charing Cross station, offering soup and sandwiches prepared by his mother, Ada. Through these experiences Steve began to develop the deep sense of social awareness, and the need for social justice, which were to underpin so much of what he was to do in later years. Even in his boyhood years, Steve had seen enough of the pain and inequalities of life in the inner city to know that he must do something about them. It was out of these burning convictions that the vision was formed in his mind of a hostel, a school and a hospital, each run by Christians, to begin to redress the injustices and lack of opportunities suffered by so many. Although he would not have understood the words, he was already visualising the concept of 'holistic ministry', the whole Gospel for the whole person, body, mind and spirit.

It was, however, the truth of God's love for the world which consumed his mind after that crucial Friday evening when he committed his life to Christ. Before long, at the age of 15, he was playing in a band and speaking at events led by Steve Flashman, then a student of Spurgeon's College. He wanted to tell people about his faith but was advised that he still had much to learn, and that to be effective he should obtain some training as soon as he left school. To Steve, what better place could there be than Spurgeons College just a short distance up the hill from where he lived? The college had, after all, conducted the mission at which he had faced up to the claims of the Gospel. So Steve needed little convincing that Spurgeons was the place to go. Moreover, he was convinced that the Baptist ministry would give him the ideal platform from which he could tell others about Christ. However, several years were to pass before his hopes were realised. After completing but failing his A-levels, Steve lived for two years with Steve Flashman, by now the minister of South Ashford Baptist Church, earning his keep in a manual job and assisting the pastor by running the youth group and speaking as opportunities arose.

The time came for him to apply to Spurgeons College. In the event, the College Council were less accommodating than Steve had hoped. It advised the now impatient applicant that he needed more experience before embarking on the training for which he yearned. As a result,

Steve spent a year working at Gravesend Baptist Church, Kent, under the guidance of Rev. David Beer, before embarking on a 3 year Diploma of Theology course at the College. David had been asked by the College to "take this young man and sit on him", but had wisely decided to do the opposite and to give Steve the freedom and scope he needed to develop his potential. Following the successful completion of the course in 1980, Steve went on, as was often the practice, to complete a year of Pastoral Studies. However, his heart was in evangelism and much of his time was spent in the pubs of London evangelising in conjunction with a band led by his friend, Keith Loring. His preoccupation with this, and his efforts to set up a trust called Anagram in association with Youth for Christ, led a senior member of the academic staff to observe that, to get Steve to attend pastoral lectures, the timetable needed to be set in line with his availability, rather than the other way round!

Steve began his final year at Spurgeons by marrying Cornelia on 23 August. Cornelia's parents had fled as refugees from the abortive Hungarian revolution in 1956, when she was a toddler. Notwithstanding her Catholic upbringing, Cornelia had become a member of the Holmesdale Road Church's youth club and there the couple met for the first time. Corni, as she is affectionately known by her friends, was not only to became Steve's wife but also, in due course, the mother of their four children, Emily, Daniel, Abigail and Joshua.

Following her marriage, Cornelia was quickly pitched into a role that was totally unfamiliar to her. She had become a Christian at the age of 21, but she had little knowledge of Baptist church life or of what was required of her as the wife of a Baptist student and evangelist. During her first year of marriage she sometimes felt ill at ease as she tried to understand the role she was expected to play. The years that followed showed that her fears were understandable but ill founded. In the story which follows, Cornelia is the key but silent player. None of what was achieved through Oasis would have been possible without her loving, faithful and self-effacing ministry as she cared for the family and provided Steve with the love and security at home which he needed: a refuge from the incessant pressures of the public life and ministry to which God had called him.

13

Steve was the driving force behind the development of Oasis over the years. However, as the following pages will show, God added others at the right time and with the right skills and experience, to develop and take forward the work, to enable it to grow and to have an impact, not just in the UK, but also across the world.

Chapter 2
Formative Days

"God stinks" exclaimed the young preacher as he got into his stride one Sunday morning. Quickly recognising his slip of the tongue, Steve tried again. "Sin stinks" he cried, as he went on to preach a sermon sufficiently good to convince the normally conservative members of Tonbridge Baptist Church (TBC) that he was worth taking on as their Assistant Minister. He was at last a minister in his own right, able to challenge young and old with the claims of the Gospel.

So, in a sense, began the story of Oasis. However, as explained above, ever since becoming a Christian, Steve had felt God's call to share the Gospel with others and to help those less fortunate than himself. During his time in Gravesend, David Beer had seen his potential to challenge people, and particularly young people, with the truths of the Christian message. David had subsequently moved to Tonbridge and had persuaded TBC that here was a young man who had the gifts for which the church was looking at that time. Steve joined in September 1981, and the years which followed saw the development of various initiatives piloting many of the projects and programmes undertaken by Oasis in the years to come.

Steve had often remarked on the importance of not only 'what' was said to people about the Gospel but also 'how' it was said, reflecting the words of Jesus in John chapter 12 v 49, "....but the Father who sent me commanded me what to say and how to say it". The way in which the Church communicated its message, particularly to young people, became a primary focus of his ministry. Young people were, even then, leaving the church in large numbers. Steve began to call on churches of all denominations to find ways of bridging the ever-widening gap between the constantly changing youth culture and the conservative, even staid, approaches of the established denominations.

Thus, in the laboratory of Tonbridge, Steve experimented with methods of communicating the Gospel. In those days, these were strikingly original. One of his early initiatives was to take over the local bus station and to use videos, pop music, and other modern means of communication to reach many hundreds, even thousands, of young people in a setting and manner compatible with their culture and interests. The 'Video Express' was to become a key tool in early Oasis Missions.

In 1984, the young people of the church set up the 'Beggars Banquet' restaurant in Tonbridge High Street. The aim was to raise money by providing, unusually, third world meals at first world prices, and inviting diners to 'Eat Less and Pay More.' The intention was to draw attention to the needs of the developing world and to encourage churchgoers and non-churchgoers alike to address the glaring inequalities which existed between the richer and the poorer nations. The project raised enough money to enable Tear Fund to sink five water wells in India and, because of its success, was run nationally by Oasis in 1989. Perhaps more important, the project provided a key launching pad for the expansion of Oasis work abroad in the 1990s. Following 'Beggars Banquet' the young people set up a radio station in Tonbridge High Street broadcasting to the local community and raising funds through dedications and donations. These projects were the forerunners of many future projects under the name 'Christmas Cracker'.

It was also in Tonbridge that Steve first saw the possibilities for fulfilling his boyhood vision for a hostel for homeless people. Contacts were made and possibilities explored within the town, but Steve soon became convinced that the hostel should operate in the inner city and not in the leafy streets of a Kentish town. Thus the seeds of the Oasis Social Care and Community programmes of later years were sown.

Steve had always felt that Christians tended to treat the media as a threat, rather than as an opportunity to speak effectively about their faith. In 1983-84 he therefore accepted an invitation by Invicta Radio, a local radio station, to host an early morning religious programme on Sunday mornings. This involved getting up at 5.00 am to be in the studio in time for the broadcast. Although he did not know it at the time, the experience enabled him to cut his teeth on the challenges of broadcasting and to develop those skills which were to prove so important in later years. Perhaps equally important, Steve learnt to discipline himself and to engage in those physically and mentally punishing schedules which were to become a normal part of his life and ministry.

But it was his call to evangelism that became, perhaps, the most pervasive influence on Steve's early ministry. In August 1985, after four years at TBC, he accepted an invitation to serve as the National Youth Evangelist for the Baptist Union. The Baptist Superintendent for Kent, Rev. Bill Hancock, had advised Steve to take every opportunity to develop his gifts and to broaden his ministry beyond that of the local church. Steve accepted this perceptive advice and Oasis became, for a short time, effectively the youth arm of the Baptist Union.

It soon became clear to Steve, as he travelled the country, that he could not evangelise the world on his own, nor resolve, by himself, the social injustices represented by the homeless on the streets of London. Calling on the analogy of a fireman with a bucket of water, wondering how to put out a major fire when all the other firemen were asleep, he chose to pour the water over the 'sleeping firemen': that is, to wake them up, and to recruit others to help him to evangelise and re-invigorate dead or dying urban churches. The first such church was Westbourne Park Baptist Church, Paddington, a church occupying huge but nearly empty premises. The church had seen better days and now badly needed the infusion of new life and resources. Meanwhile, certain possibilities for setting up a home for homeless people began to emerge.

As early as 1985, it was becoming clear that Steve needed a support structure to assist him with the ministries in which he was beginning to engage. Having recognised the possibilities for evangelism and social action in London, a small group of friends and fellow members in the church in Tonbridge came together to form a charitable trust to assist in the provision of financial and other support. A small trust called 'The Ranch Charitable Trust' was adopted, with Julia Honey, William Matheson, Andy Simmonds and Philip Warland as Trustees. William Matheson, a London solicitor and one-time Chairman of Interserve, a large and well-established mission agency, was appointed Chairman.

17

The name of the Trust was subsequently changed to Oasis. Cornelia, Steve's wife, suggested the name because she saw the hoped-for home for homeless young people as an oasis from the rigours and deprivation of street life. In the event, the Trust provided the legal framework within which all the activities and ministries of Oasis were to develop in subsequent years. Little did the trustees realise that under the guidance of God they were establishing a ministry that would reach not just the confines of London but other cities across the world.

The first formal meeting of the re-named Trust was held in October 1986. Philip Warland was elected Chairman in succession to William Matheson, and Nikky Mungeam, a 17-year-old member of the Tonbridge Baptist Youth Group, was taken on as Steve's full-time secretary. Much of the discussion in these early days centred on legal questions and how to support and pay Steve, Nikky, and the first volunteer team recently based in Paddington. The agenda also dealt with the Chalke family's need for housing and aspects of employment law. These were issues which were to arise frequently during the early days of the Trust. A decision was also taken to issue a quarterly prayer letter to the small but growing group of people who had begun to support the work in various ways.

The early emphasis on evangelism or 'Introducing people to Jesus' (the first Oasis strap line), lead to a natural affinity between Oasis and the Hildenborough Evangelistic Trust, which had been set up to support the work of the evangelist Tom Rees and a Christian holiday and Conference Centre, (now Otford Manor in Kent, owned by Oak Hall Holidays). In early 1987 a programme of joint projects was agreed and there was some discussion about the possibility of a merger between the two Trusts. However, the strong emphasis of Oasis on programmes of social action requiring substantial funding did not lie comfortably with the primary purpose of the Hildenborough Trust - to use its funds for evangelism purposes - and the merger did not take place. Oasis was nonetheless indebted to the Trust for the help which it gave in a number of ways, but particularly by assisting with certain salary costs and providing a home for Steve and his family in Forest Hill, close to central London.

1987 was a key year in the Trust's early development. Oasis moved its small office in Tonbridge to Chatsworth Road Baptist Church in South London. Ruth Clinch, a retired missionary from Zaire, was

local denominations as wished to be involved. 22 locations were visited in the weeks between 20 November and 16 December 1989.

The project was overseen by a Steering Committee made up of representatives of the main denominations and other Christian bodies, including Youth for Christ. The Bible Society also sat on the Group and played a key role in training, whilst Spring Harvest and others, including the Christian Publicity Organisation, gave support.

All these activities however involved considerable costs - costs it was hoped would be offset by registration fees and sales of resource materials and merchandise. In the event, the cost of the national tour and a shortfall in registration income meant that the project began to build up unsustainable deficits almost from day one. One of the problems was that many churches took up the ideas of Christmas Unwrapped and ran projects without paying the Registration fee. In terms of the project's objectives this was to be commended, but it left a big hole in the finances of Oasis which, at that stage in its life, it was ill equipped to bear.

On the positive (and more important) side, many thousands of people were introduced to the gospel and many became Christians. The records show that over 500 churches registered to take part in the first year, plus an unquantifiable number of non-registered participants who had responded to the national media campaign. There were many other benefits, particularly in the way churches worked together, and individuals were built up in their faith.

At the popular level, Cliff Richard's Christmas single, 'Saviour's Day', written by Chris Eaton, hit Number 1 in the charts, but to the disappointment of the Unwrapped team was not marketed under the Christmas Unwrapped brand as they had hoped.

Oasis always sought to evaluate its projects and then to decide whether to repeat them or to move on. A survey of participants showed how successful the project had been and it was hoped to extend it to a second year. However, the finances of the project were such that the decision was reluctantly taken to put it on to a care and maintenance basis. As events turned out, although a number of churches engaged in the project in 1991, the time had come for Oasis to move to other things.

On Fire

By initiating and resourcing a nationwide project across denominations and organisational boundaries, Christmas Unwrapped marked an important development in the Trust's approach to evangelism. It addressed the question "How can we get people to notice the fact that Christians have a message to give, and how can we get them within earshot?" Too often in the past, committed and well-intentioned churches had run 'missions', but the number of outsiders attending would often be disappointingly low. The project showed, however, that evangelism or 'introducing people to Jesus' could best be done by encouraging the churches to leave their 'ghettos' and to reach out locally to the people round about them. The aim should be to build bridges to make it easier for people to understand the Christian message by experiencing, as well as hearing about, the love of Christ, hitherto mainly proclaimed from the pulpit.

Despite Christmas Unwrapped, Oasis continued to be challenged by the limited impact of so much evangelistic activity, including its own. Before long it was asking itself again whether there were other ways in which the vital objective of reaching others could be achieved.

By September 1991 a new idea had emerged which Steve reported to the Trustees. In concept it was not dissimilar to Christmas Unwrapped though there were many lessons which had to be learned and applied for it to be more effective. Once again it would be a national project with a local emphasis. This time, however, the activities would centre on Pentecost, the birthday of the Christian Church - the day when the Holy Spirit was poured out on the disciples, giving them the power to be bold and effective witnesses of Jesus Christ. 'On Fire', as it came to be called, offered churches a way to celebrate that birthday, and a stirring new hymn was written by Paul Field for the occasion. However, the celebrations were not to be limited to in-church activities but would be designed to involve the whole community. It was recognised that very few people did not enjoy a party - whatever the reason for the celebration - and a party to celebrate the birthday of the Church may be no exception.

So plans were made for hundreds, perhaps thousands, of parties up and down the country, to be held on Saturday, 21 May 1994. Local communities would be invited to join in the celebrations organised by

The holistic approach to mission was becoming increasingly apparent and established.

Oasis' evaluation of the "On Fire" project showed that perhaps as many as 2000 churches were involved while the youth arm, 'Fired Up' raised approximately £80,000 for children at risk worldwide. These figures are, however, only proxy indicators of the influence of the projects on the churches involved, their local communities, and on the lives of many thousands of young people who faced up to the problems of poverty in the developing world, many for the first time.

Fanfare

Following 'On Fire' a significant change in the level of Oasis mission activity occurred. Dennis Pethers left Oasis to start a new evangelistic organisation 'Viz a Viz', Peter Staley moved back into church work and Simon Parish moved across to support Steve in the administration and management of his now extensive range of ministries. These became increasingly concentrated on the media - TV, radio, books, journals and newspapers. (see chapter 10).

By 1998 Oasis in the UK was nonetheless beginning to think about the opportunities for communicating the gospel presented by the new Millennium. An NOP poll in 1996, into attitudes and beliefs in the resurrection, had shown that despite the Decade of Evangelism and despite the resources put into evangelism by Oasis and others, while 70 per cent of people in the UK claimed to be Christian only around ten per cent attended church regularly. Church membership had fallen in the first half of the 1990s, with all the main churches having seen a drop in their 'market share'. In the light of this, Steve Chalke posed the question "Do we throw in the towel and admit defeat or do we rise to the challenge and debunk the media myth that churches are often out of touch and irrelevant?"

Answering his own question, Steve conceived with others an especially tailored project 'Fanfare for a New Generation' embracing a wide range of organisations including All Souls, Langham Place, the Cliff Richard organisation, the Evangelical Alliance, the Bible Society, March for Jesus, and the Archbishop's Millennium Advisory Group.

The project was focused on the first Sunday of the new Millennium, 2 January 2000. In the morning the emphasis was to be on activities by local churches as they sought to attract people into church, perhaps for the first time for many years, thereby starting the new Millennium by acknowledging the God in whom 70 per cent claimed they believed. In the evening the new Millennium was celebrated in a concert given by the All Souls orchestra conducted by Noel Tredinnick. Around these focal points, and in support of them, the 'Fanfare' team, directed by Sue Radford, produced a range of strategic resources to help local churches to build bridges with their local communities; to encourage people to 'try' their local church; and to equip local churches to adopt 'outsider friendly' services. Oasis had earlier had dealings with Willow Creek Community Church in Chicago and drew on some of its ideas.

A particular effort was made to develop the role of the church in local schools. This initiative, named 'Generation to Generation', was developed by Oasis in cooperation with Scripture Union in Schools, CARE for Education, the Schools' Ministry Network, Agape and others. It involved a wide range of activities from buying new football kits and computers to the development of prayer networks and involvement in local school boards, PTAs and other school based groups.

All three national projects run in the 1990s emphasised the importance of the church being involved in the local community, all involved close cooperation between churches and Christian organisations, and all provided advice and resources for those who felt the time had come seriously to challenge the decline of the church in the late 20th century.

Mission and the New Technologies

At the same time Oasis had been thinking about reaching people through the new technologies, and early in the new Century it introduced the concept of the 'virtual' church to be found on line at 'Church.co.uk'. This was a one-stop shop for people wanting to explore the Christian faith on the Internet and discover what the message of Jesus was really about. The site offered a wide range of interactive services to enable people to ask questions, to explore difficult issues, and to acquire helpful resources.

Another initiative with a similar object was the creation of Xalt.co.uk, an Internet service provider and a source of further infor-

Number 3 Cerise Road

It took some five years from the formal setting up of Oasis Trust in 1985 for the vision for the hostel to be fulfilled. The story is one which demonstrates how God works in remarkable ways to achieve His purposes, and it is one which has been repeated in different contexts throughout the life of the Trust.

By the beginning of 1985, despite considerable efforts, no suitable premises had been found either in the inner city of London or elsewhere. The problems seemed formidable, not least because Steve was beginning to travel the country as an evangelist and money was scarce. One day in the summer of 1985 whilst on holiday, Steve received a phone call from Noel Fawcett, the Associate Pastor at Rye Lane Chapel, Peckham in south London. The call was of enormous significance. Noel said that he had heard that Steve was looking for premises, suitable for use as a hostel, and that No. 3 Cerise Road was coming on to the market. The house was severely dilapidated but had been used previously to house female employees of Sainsbury's. Although this was the kind of call Steve had been hoping and praying for over the years, in practice he was ill prepared or equipped to take on such a major undertaking. However, in discussion with friends at the church and having spent some months learning about hostels, Steve agreed that the best way to proceed was to form a charity through which funds could be raised to purchase the property and support his ministry as an evangelist. It was felt at the time that if the house could be acquired it could also be used as Steve and Cornelia's home, thus facilitating his intended move to London.

By March 1987, the Trust's minutes record that an offer on number 3 Cerise Road, Peckham had been accepted, but planning permission was still needed for the extensive renovation which was required. Permission was obtained in time for the Trustees' September meeting, but the necessary funds were still not forthcoming. However, in July 1987, the Trustees were told that the Baptist Union, acting on behalf of a private trust, the Woodlands Trust, were offering Oasis the use of a house in Croydon (in the south-west suburbs of London) which would be suitable as a hostel and offices. Moreover, Steve had been approached by one, Mrs Mary Scroggie, the daughter-in-law of Dr. Graham Scroggie, and a Trustee of Woodlands Trust, saying that if

Oasis took the house in Croydon, she would make a donation of £5,000. She had heard Steve preach and had been moved by what he had said.

In view of the absence of significant funds to enable Oasis to purchase the house in Peckham, the offer was seen as both extremely generous and, at first sight, very attractive in a number of respects. However, when it was discussed in depth, it was decided to turn it down on the grounds that the property was not in the Inner City and was not therefore in line with Steve's vision, or the aims of the Trust. The Trustees wondered, however, if the property in Croydon could be sold and the proceeds used to purchase No. 3 Cerise Road. Shortly after this Mrs Scroggie rang Steve to say that the Trustees of the Woodlands Trust had decided to sell the property in Croydon and give the proceeds, some £187,000, to Oasis. By February 1988 the Croydon property was on the market and by June of that year contracts had been exchanged.

The property in Peckham looked like an ordinary terraced house but there was extensive living space to the rear. Rather than call the house 'The Oasis Hostel' it was decided to use the more neutral name 'No. 3' because it was known that many street people were averse to the idea of 'hostel' living. The Trust's aim was to make No. 3 a real home.

Planning for the new project could now get seriously under way and a project group was formed under the guidance of Barry Lock, who at that time was an Area Manager for Social Services in Kent. One of the group's first tasks was to prepare a project specification. It was decided that No. 3 should be 'a medium-stay referred access hostel' offering accommodation and independence training for single homeless people aged 16 to 25 years. In this context 'medium stay' meant one year; 'referred access' meant 'referred from another agency', (i.e., not taken off the street); and 'independence training' meant two phases of six months each, progressively enabling residents to increase their capacity for independent living prior to departure.

The hostel was opened in February 1990 with Mrs Scroggie as Guest of Honour. It had taken three years to acquire and had cost over £350,000, including extensive refurbishment, furniture and equipment. During this time it was occupied by Fi McLachlan, Oasis Director of Social Care and other Oasis staff, although it had been thought initially that it would provide accommodation for Steve. The facilities offered accommodation for up to ten young people - five in rooms with communal living facilities in phase 1, and five independent units for phase 2 with cooking facilities and separate metered electricity. Each resident was allocated to a 'key worker'. This was a residential staff member responsible for meeting regularly with the young person and formulating a personal independence-training plan appropriate to the person concerned. The plan included training in such matters as personal hygiene, cooking, job-hunting, links with the family, budgeting, and education and training opportunities.

Whatever the planned modus operandi of the hostel, its success or failure essentially rested on the quality of the team which was appointed to run the project. Dave Nwokedi, led the team of three support workers under the direction of Fi McLachlan who had overseen the development of all aspects of the project since May 1989. The four permanent workers provided 24-hour cover with the help of volunteers. Dave, his wife Jill and their two children lived at the hostel and made a huge difference, contributing to the homely and friendly atmosphere which pervaded it. Dave also had a keen sense of humour. He would 'threaten' disorderly residents to the effect that if their behaviour did not improve, he would read the Bible outside their rooms in the hope that they would take its message to heart, or leave!

The running of a hostel was a new experience for all the team members and it quickly became clear that it was one thing to plan the running of a hostel, but quite another to do so successfully. Whilst the management committee had addressed all the obvious issues, there were others which arose that needed clearly thought through policies, some of which were absent or ill-defined in the early days. These centred on how the residents could be given maximum personal freedom but at the same time preserve the standards of Christian conduct to which Oasis was committed. How should drugs, violence and racism be penalised or treated and how could Oasis best handle undesirable visitors? There were frequently disturbing incidents, and prayer was constantly needed for the protection of residents and staff alike. Another issue was the extent to which the Christian faith should be presented and made available to the residents. In this it was decided that Oasis would make clear its Christian commitment but would not require residents to take part in, for instance, prayer, worship or Bible study.

It was a steep learning curve but Dave Nwokedi and his team, through Christian love, professional expertise and common sense, slowly began to take informed views of these and other issues. The first year was, nonetheless, very challenging as they sought to help severely damaged people, often refugees and people from the ethnic minorities, to find stability and self-respect.

The stories of the many who were helped are too numerous to tell here. However, that of one young woman, whom we shall call Dana, is worth telling. Taken in originally by an agency, Dana, at the age of 16, was sleeping rough in The Strand and studying simultaneously for her O levels. She was an ambitious and able young lady who hoped to be an engineer. However, through various circumstances, Dana had found herself without a home and on the streets of London. Dana was received by No. 3 and entered into phase 1 of the 12-month programme of training. As a young black woman, she was particularly vulnerable and the move to No. 3 came as a great relief. The staff were able to help her with her studies and when her O levels were completed Dana found a place at a local Further Education College. In time she left No3 and transferred into 'move on' accommodation. It is understood at the time of writing that she was successful in obtaining a qualification in a particular aspect of engineering. At the time, the government was seeking to encourage young women to take up engineering, and people from ethnic communities were struggling to achieve qualifications, often against heavy odds. Through the work of No. 3, together with that of other agencies, a young black woman had been restored to her proper place in society. More recently it transpired that a Head of the Conservative Party's PR Department had at one stage been a resident of No. 3 - a remarkable transformation.

But the ending was not always happy. On one occasion a tall and immensely strong resident drew a knife on Dave Nwokedi, and on other occasions the behaviour of residents was so bad that the ultimate sanction of exclusion had to be applied, to the great sadness of the staff. However, Dave and his team often made such a mark that evicted residents sometimes came back to thank them for their help and continued to maintain good relations. This pressure often told, especially on volunteers, and assistant staff found it difficult to stay for more than one year.

Finances were also a worry. Although the Woodlands Trust, the Baptist Union and donations to Oasis had covered the capital costs of the project, there were still recurrent costs to be met. Single homeless people were, at the time, entitled to help through a hostel deficit grant and this was obtained through a partnership with the Adullam Homes Housing Association - a Christian organisation who over time made an enormous contribution to the project, both in terms of management advice and finances. Income was sought from residents' rental payments, but this effectively depended on the good offices of the London Borough of Southwark who were responsible for housing benefit. At the time, in the early 1990s, the local authority was experiencing great difficulties in housing benefit administration and serious shortfalls in No 3's income arose as a result.

By the end of 1990, Oasis was already turning its mind to the development of an overall strategy for meeting the various needs of homeless people. Four elements emerged: the first was the need to provide more accommodation for the increasing number of homeless people on the streets of Inner London; the second was to provide a team of workers on the streets with direct access to those in need of housing accommodation; the third was the need for 'move on' accommodation to free space for new referrals; and the fourth was the need for a medical facility.

By this time, Oasis had become known as an organisation which was tackling the issues of homelessness in some depth, and not superficially seeking to remove people from the gaze of members of the public as they entered their chosen restaurant or visited West End theatres or cinemas. Political pressure was growing and agencies for the homeless needed to respond. As a result, local authorities began to show an interest in the Trust's strategy and some approached Oasis for advice and guidance. A number of bodies, including churches, offered Oasis the use of run down or surplus accommodation, but the Trust was not strong enough financially to take up these offers.

There was great satisfaction that No. 3 was up and running, but it was recognised that this was only a beginning. It was good to receive referrals from other agencies, but what the Trust really needed was a "direct access" hostel to take significant numbers of homeless people

43

directly off the streets. In 1990 it came to the notice of Fi McLachlan that the Methodist Church was selling a hostel previously used for international students in Lambeth, close to Waterloo. The Trust immediately entered into discussions with Methodist Church officials about the possibility of acquiring the premises. Simultaneously, it approached the Government which was making money available through the Department of the Environment for the crisis management of homeless people over winter months. The international centre offered 60 beds and Oasis planned to develop it into a crisis centre which would provide outreach workers, an advice and counselling centre, meals and medical facilities. Favourable signals were received both from the Methodists and the Government, but the project never came into being. A site visit was paid by Sir Michael Spicer, then a junior Minister in the Department of the Environment, but it seemed that he had little interest in seriously addressing the needs of the homeless, only getting them off the streets. The Government appeared to be looking for an occupancy rate which was higher than anything acceptable to the Trust. Whilst discussions continued, the Methodist Church decided that it could not sell the premises to Oasis at a price the Trust could afford. It had financial requirements which, understandably perhaps, were of a higher priority and it sold the tower block to the highest bidder. A number of other possibilities were explored at the time but without success. The Trust therefore turned its attention to the development of work on the streets, 'move on' accommodation, and to the provision of appropriate medical facilities.

Street Teams

The aim was to bring together teams of young people who, following training and prayer, would go on to the streets of Central London. 'Cardboard City' in Waterloo, Lincoln's Inn Fields and the Strand were notorious for accommodating those without a home. The aim was to build relationships and establish trust in order to be in a position to offer help. The first set of teams started in October 1990 with groups of between 4 and 8 people going out on five nights a week, meeting and befriending the people huddled in shop entrances, under cardboard boxes, and anywhere else where shelter could be found. The teams came from diverse church backgrounds across London but all had the common desire to be Christ to the homeless. By working to a 'beat' system, the teams got to know and to meet those who were sleeping rough on a regular basis.

Oasis provided initial training and ongoing monthly support for these volunteers. In addition, it became part of a forum of agencies who were engaged in planning and meeting the needs of the homeless in central London. Oasis also ran Christmas meals for a large number of homeless people in a building in Covent Garden, lent to the Trust by the London City Mission. These Christmas events proved very popular and were run by the street teams and other Oasis staff.

It was not long before God began to use these dedicated people to great effect. One 14 year old boy, Simon, had run away and within four days of reaching the streets had been approached by a pimp desiring his sexual services. As Simon was terrified and desperate for help, Oasis found him accommodation for the night and negotiated with his home, the Social Services, and the police, for his ongoing wellbeing.

A 30-year-old woman had left her job and was in need of counselling in respect of her past experiences. Again, having safely housed her, Oasis staff were able to arrange the help she needed, and negotiated her return to work. Over Christmas 1990 she became a Christian.

Many men on the streets had been in the Armed Forces and, for whatever reasons, had found themselves struggling and homeless. One Friday night a team member came across Dave, an ex-soldier who had seen service in many parts of the world, including the Falklands. He was now homeless and jobless. An attempt was made to move him into a hostel but, like many homeless people, he found hostel living unacceptable. Nonetheless, Dave enjoyed the tea and sandwiches brought to him every week at his patch in the Strand. He also accepted prayer and the gift of a New Testament, which he read eagerly. It was clear that he was open to God as he recounted the passages he had read, and which had meant something to him. He then asked Oasis to help him to stop drinking, which he described as 'the demon', and steps were taken to assist him down this road. Dave began to go to church with some of the team, and the changes were obvious. Earlier, in a sober moment, Dave had indicated that he used to be part of the Emmaus Community in Cambridge. The Community were happy to take Dave back and so far as Oasis is aware he has continued to keep hold of his faith and remain sober. (Note - all the names of people used in this chapter have been changed to protect their identity.)

These are just a few of the many stories which could be told. In helping to bring about change in the lives of those concerned, Christian workers were in constant competition with people who, in some cases, were out to exploit the most vulnerable members of society. There were many wolves in sheep's clothing who offered homeless people love and support, only to ensnare them in vice, drugs and slavery.

It soon became clear that a vehicle to support the teams on the streets would be an invaluable asset. Such a vehicle - a double-decker bus - became available through the good offices of a supporter. The bus, which had previously served as a clubhouse for a sailing club on a gravel pit, was painted with the Oasis logo on its side, and became a well-known feature on the streets of Central London. It provided a place to talk, to offer food and hot drinks, and to store blankets and sleeping bags, all essential supplies for those sleeping rough. In due time a replacement bus was required and a vehicle was given to Oasis by Stagecoach.

Whilst the vehicles proved a great asset, they were also a constant liability. First, there was the need for qualified drivers, an ongoing problem, which sometimes limited the extent to which they could be used. The second major problem was parking. There were few places in Central London where the bus could be parked, but this issue was partially resolved by NCP's offer to accommodate the bus first close to Liverpool Street station, and later in a coach park in Battersea. This involved considerable time and expense for staff getting to and fro and it was greatly to the credit of Ian Lees and Julia Turner, the Social Care Administrator, that the Mobile Care Unit, as it came to be known, remained in operation. The third liability was the cost of running and maintenance. Some of these costs were met by the Maidstone and District Bus Company who offered to do the servicing, but in the main they were a charge on the general funds.

The work at No. 3, the street teams and the mobile care unit touched a real chord with the churches, and the Christian public generally. Some churches attended training weekends put on by Oasis to stimulate work across the country. Children took part in an innovative project called 'Screepers' through which they collected toothbrushes, soap and other necessary toiletries. Numerous fundraising efforts were

46

organised including 'sleep outs' in Central London when people entered, however briefly, into the experience of sleeping rough.

In due course the London Borough of Southwark recognised the work of Oasis by providing funding towards No.3's running costs: referring homeless young people to the Trust; and by providing 'move on' accommodation to supplement that provided by Oasis itself. Oasis had won the right to be taken seriously by the authorities.

Montrell Road

It had always been intended that 'move on' accommodation should be provided so that the transition to normal independent life for those leaving No.3 would be managed and smooth. The idea was to acquire a large property which could be used as flats and to appoint a residential caretaker to give support to the tenants. In 1992 Streatham Baptist Church approached Oasis with a view to developing such a project. No.24 Montrell Road, Streatham had come to the notice of the church. The property was owned by the City Parochial Foundation and had for many years been leased to the Knights Association who wished to relinquish the lease. With the help of a number of churches, trusts and foundations, plus a loan from the Baptist Union Corporation, Oasis was able to purchase the property and to undertake the necessary refurbishment work. It was designed to accommodate 9 young people between the ages of 16 and 25 who would be able to live virtually independently with the help of a project worker living on site.

No. 24 was opened on 1 November 1995 in the year of Oasis' 10th Anniversary. Barry Lock, now Director of Social Care, commented that the new project was "an integral part of Steve's original vision ..... as one project (No 3) has given the impetus for another (No 24)". He went on to lay down the following challenge, which remains with Oasis to this day, "We must never become complacent, accepting homelessness as a fact of life. We must keep in the front of our minds the potential for change and go on challenging people to ensure that the plight of homeless people is not ignored".

Elizabeth Baxter Health Centre

Whilst much was now in place, it was evident that street living also took a serious toll on the health of homeless people. They were subject both to the normal illnesses experienced by the generality of the population and to particular ailments associated with their way of life - problems with feet, skin conditions and TB were commonplace. There were also the ongoing problems of alcohol and drug addiction, some of which were the cause of homelessness, while in other cases they offered the only respite available for the pain of isolation, rejection and hopelessness experienced on the streets. Although statutory agencies, including the NHS, were ostensibly there to meet these needs, the harsh reality of the time meant that hospitals would not always admit people who were dirty and living on the streets and, it has to be said, many street people were unwilling to seek help from these agencies because of the way in which they were often received.

Oasis believed that one of the most effective ways of meeting the needs of homeless people, apart from providing accommodation, would be a medical centre offering services that the NHS could not, or would not, provide. It was against this background that a call was received one afternoon from the Editorial Director of the Christian Herald enquiring whether Oasis had any use for a derelict building, the Elizabeth Baxter Hostel, located opposite the Imperial War Museum close to the heart of London. The building had taken its name from the wife of the Christian Herald's founder, Michael Paget Baxter who, in 1927, had had his attention drawn to "the large number of homeless people to be found huddled in the nooks and crannies of the Embankment, and the bridges which span the Thames. Michael Baxter immediately set out to befriend and help as many people as he could, using his own resources and donations sent by readers. In addition to providing food and shelter to homeless men, a hostel for young women was set up under the care of Mr Baxter's granddaughter, another Elizabeth Baxter, who dedicated her life to continuing his mission to the poor and the destitute".[1]

The Grade II listed building needed well over £250,000 for its restoration. The Trustees of the hostel, who were located in Hastings,

[1] Extract from the Christian Herald 24 April 1983

Steve and Cornelia on their wedding day

Steve's ministry – early days

Ruth Clinch

Shout Theatre Company

Dennis Pethers and the videowall

Renovation of No. 3 Cerise Road

No. 3 resident and Abbe Stapleton in key work session

Mobile Care Unit in action

Elizabeth Baxter Health Centre

Four residents at No.3 are now working and others are starting college in the Autumn, which is very encouraging for

Frank Field visited No.3. They met with residents and talked to staff about Oasis' work with homeless people.

members. Staff were able to help him, and to thereby deepen the trust he has in them.

For more information on Oasis Social Care, please contact Penny Sertin on 0171 450 9000

Start
for Excluded Pupils

'hat was the message
it took power last
ipils are permanently
nds more at risk.
96 to support young
ded from school, or
'at risk of' exclusion

an insecure, vulnerable and often damaged individual."

Fresh Start does much of its work in small groups. Through group exercises, Fresh Start aims to get the young people listening to each other and developing their own communication skills.

The project also places a great emphasis on mentoring - a process by which an older and more

Arthur Brown and Fresh Start

the theological under-pinning of the venture as it was a far cry from their traditional concept of mission. This may explain why the number of churches actually involved in the project was significantly fewer than the number expressing interest at the outset.

The Croydon Council also changed its position. Whilst accepting the challenge which had been set by Oasis, they put forward an alternative proposal. They would provide a site and a new building provided Oasis and the churches raised the money to pay for it - a figure of £500,000. Oasis agreed to this on the basis that if they succeeded in raising the money, it would run the hostel in association with the churches of Croydon.

The project was launched by a number of celebrities at the Whitgift Centre, Croydon, at the end of September 1998. The Christian press represented the project as a challenge to Christian young people; local Croydon newspapers represented the leader of the council as challenging all the young people of Croydon to play their part; church youth leaders saw the project as young people in Croydon helping young people in Croydon. The mission statement did not mention the churches but read as follows:

"RAW is training, equipping, mobilising and empowering the young people of Croydon to work together in partnership with the Council and other agencies as part of 'Croydon United'. RAW is young people using their raw talents and energy to help other young people achieve their full potential, enabling them to be active, responsible members of the community." Summarised, it challenged the young people of Croydon as to whether they wanted to 'make history' or 'be history'.

The hostel itself was designed to draw on the lessons learned from No. 3 and to follow the Foyer model for hostels which was currently in vogue. Like No. 3, it was to be a medium stay hostel with twelve to fifteen beds for people between 16 and 25. It would also offer high levels of support, training in life skills and preparation for independence. Christians would run it all day every day for 365 days of the year. Although Oasis and its partner churches were unable to raise the original target of £500,000, a significant sum was raised and the hostel opened in July 2000 under the auspices of a partnership consisting of Oasis, the Broomleigh Housing Association and the London Borough of Croydon.

In the latter stages of the project, interest dwindled amongst the churches, but a number maintained their interest and support throughout. The extent to which the community became involved in the life of the churches was less than had been hoped. Various initiatives were taken to involve unchurched young people in church fundraising projects - similar to those which had proved successful with Christmas Cracker, but with limited success.

Although the churches of Croydon assisted in setting up the Foyer Hostel, now run and managed by Oasis, it could be argued that they failed fully to grasp the nature of the new form of mission. Nor, it appears, did they fully understand the benefits to the community of a close working relationship with the local authority. Both of these weaknesses were to be addressed later in the 'Faithworks' project. Despite these reservations the impressive new hostel provided another haven for the homeless young people of London.

Conclusion

Throughout the entire development of the Oasis Social Care Programme, the words of Jesus Christ in Matthew 25:35, 36 & 40 were always present, *"For I was hungry and you gave me something to eat, I was thirsty and you gave me something to drink, I was a stranger and you invited me in, I needed clothes and you clothed me, I was sick and you looked after me, I was in prison and you came to visit me"... "I tell you the truth, whatever you did for one of the least of these brothers of mine, you did for me."*

Chapter 5
Oasis School: Vision or Mirage?

Steve's vision of a secondary school in the Inner City, managed and run by Christians was at the heart of Oasis thinking from its earliest days. Soon after he left Tonbridge, Steve discussed his vision with Graham Mungeam, a member of Tonbridge Baptist Church and, at that time, an official in the Department of Education and Science (as it was then). Steve also began a search for suitable premises in London where his vision might be realised.

Graham was well placed to observe the policies being introduced first, by the then Secretary of State, the late Sir Keith Joseph, and subsequently by Kenneth Baker, now Lord Baker. He had himself been involved in the development of the Technical and Vocational Education Initiative (TVEI), which led to the concept of the City Technology College (CTC) and, more recently, the City Academy. He also oversaw programmes in educational authorities throughout England to assist "lower attaining pupils" - those pupils who did not succeed in national examinations - and the Micro-electronics Education Programme, which introduced computers and computer assisted learning into English schools. These and other Government initiatives were designed to help young people succeed at school and make a successful transition from school to working life.

In October1986 the Government announced that it was planning to set up a CTC in Peckham, South London, at the very heart of the area in which Oasis was beginning to operate. Graham met the Department's Permanent Secretary who encouraged him to take the matter up with the Head of the responsible Division and with the Special Advisor to the Secretary of State. Following an exchange of correspondence, a meeting took place in March 1988 at which Steve Chalke, accompanied by Philip Warland and several of the Trustees, discussed the possibilities with Graham and other Government advisors.

The Department responded positively to the interest shown by Oasis and suggested that it might be able to help the Trust find a sponsor for the £1million which was the minimum sum needed to start a CTC. Oasis would be expected to find £1 million or 20% of the capital costs of any project, but the school's running costs would be provided by the Government.

The officials also pointed out that the churches had not in general responded favourably to the Government's CTC proposals, perhaps because they were highly visible and controversial. Oasis pointed out that as a Christian organisation it would want to find sponsors who shared its Christian ethos and who were not politically motivated.

Following the meeting, visits were made to a number of potential sites. As early as 1987, Oasis had made enquiries of The Inner London Education Authority's Director of Education about the availability of possible sites. This had proved unfruitful, partly because of the antagonism of the Local Education Authorities (LEAs) to the Government's proposals. Before long the ILEA was abolished and the responsibility for education given to the London Boroughs.

Despite the co-operation of the Department, the difficulties were formidable and became more so when the Government announced that it had opted to transform an existing school near Peckham to a CTC. State education was still largely in the hands of local education authorities, although changes were in the pipeline which would, in due course, offer a role for the voluntary sector.

In September 1988 Steve wrote to Graham recognising that the invitation that he had put to Graham to leave the Civil Service and to help set up a school was no longer realistic. He suggested however that he might be prepared to join Oasis in the wider role of Executive Director to release Steve to carry out the ministries to which he felt called.

On taking up the post a year later, Graham sought to explore again what, if any, new possibilities existed for the development of a secular school designed to meet the needs of the inner city. He sought the interest and advice of Her Majesty's Inspectors of Schools (HMI) and introduced them to the UK Frontline Team training programme. It was apparent however that, despite its good intentions, Oasis did not have the resources, skills or experience to set up a school, let alone run one. Moreover, the political framework, though now more conducive than before, still did not offer the realistic possibility of substantial government financial assistance and backup. There was no option but to put the matter on the back burner, at least for the time being.

In January 1994, Graham told Steve that he was planning to get a group of educationalists together to consider the possibilities of setting up a school along the lines envisaged several years before. The changes in government legislation provided a clear opening that would enable Oasis to run a secular school with Christian values and, it was hoped, provide a model for schooling in the inner city. The first step was to make contact with sympathetic professionals to explore the direction the project should take.

Following discussions with a number of senior educational experts, including the Chief Inspector of Hampshire LEA, a number of head teachers, academics and senior schools administrators, it became clear that Oasis still lacked the credibility which it required if it were to be trusted with such a major project involving large amounts of tax payers money. The leadership agreed, therefore, to explore projects that would involve the Trust in educational matters and help it to gain standing in the eyes of the educational authorities.

At least three possibilities were on offer. The first was participation in the "Cities in Schools" initiative, an approach first developed in the United States, which was being introduced in inner London. Under this scheme members of the local community were invited to play a role in the running of local schools and to develop extra curricular activities.

Alternatively, Oasis could offer external moral and teaching support to primary schools in inner city areas. Many such schools were struggling at the time, and there was reliable research evidence that indicated that well-targeted help could make a significant difference to the wellbeing of children in such schools, and particularly to their performance when they entered the secondary phase.

The third option arose as a possible response to disturbing developments that were beginning to emerge in primary and secondary schools throughout the country. School 'exclusions' (expulsions) were rising rapidly and were threatening the educational opportunities of an increasing number of pupils. Perhaps, reflected the Leadership, Oasis should try to assist those pupils who had been excluded from school or even better, help those who were on the margins of exclusion before it was too late. Many such pupils were to be found in inner London, especially, but not exclusively, amongst the black ethnic minorities.

Although all three projects offered the prospect of involvement in schools, Graham recommended to the Leadership that the needs of excluded pupils and those on the margins of exclusion should be given priority over others. The numbers were increasing rapidly and the problem was being exacerbated by the greater freedom being given to some schools to exclude pupils irrespective of the consequences. The government was responding by setting up pupil referral units (PRUs) for the separate education of those who had been excluded, and legislation meant that all local authorities had to make some provision for these pupils, almost irrespective of its quality.

Moreover, the problem was on Oasis' doorstep. There were two such pupils in Haddon Hall church where the Oasis office was located, and within a short distance of the office were some of the most difficult inner city schools in the London Borough of Southwark. It seemed to the Oasis leadership that it could make a significant difference to the lives of these young people if it sought to address this problem, working in partnership with the schools concerned.

If the project was to get underway, two conditions needed to be met. First, any work in the State sector would need the support of the Local Education Authorities concerned. Second, substantial financial backing would be needed.

It seemed obvious that as the Oasis offices were located in the London Borough of Southwark, and as it was committed to work in the inner city, an early approach to the local authority would be appropriate. Through the good offices of Simon Hughes, MP for Southwark and Bermondsey and the Rev. Bruce Stokes, a Borough Dean and Minister of Brandon Baptist Church in Camberwell, a meeting was arranged between Oasis and the Chairman of the Southwark Education Committee. The Chairman responded well to the idea and suggested that Graham Mungeam should meet the LEA's Chief Education Officer to discuss the details. As a result of this meeting the CEO agreed to provide Oasis with full access to a wide range of officials dealing with the problem.

Equipped with this authority, Graham began to sound out the reaction, first of the newly formed Pupil Exclusion Unit in Peckham, and then those officials chiefly involved in exclusion issues, including Education Welfare Officers, Educational Psychologists and curricular experts. He was extremely well received and Oasis was encouraged to press on with its plans. It was made clear, however, that in the strained state of budgets at the time, little or no money would be forthcoming from the local authority.

Graham decided therefore to explore whether finance might be available through any of the range of initiatives emanating from central government. However, most central government money was at that time fed to the schools via the LEAs and was already earmarked for particular purposes. The one programme that did appear to offer possibilities was the financial support given to youth workers in schools through the Department's Youth Service Unit.

After taking soundings to ascertain that an Oasis bid would qualify for consideration, a full submission was prepared on the project. The basic idea was for Oasis young people to get alongside young people who had been excluded from school, or who were at risk of being excluded because of their bad behaviour. Oasis staff and volunteers would interact with pupils on a one to one and group basis, seeking to help, encourage and guide those who were not succeeding at school and who were disrupting the education of their fellow pupils. The emphasis would be on managing individual and group behaviour. It was hoped that personal interaction between pupils and young people with similar interests and sharing the same youth culture might break down the hostility between the young people and the 'authority figures' at the school. For instance, it was hoped (and experience proved it to be possible) that pupils could be taught to play the guitar and other musical instruments; also, they could be persuaded to participate in youth activities outside school hours. The aim was to build confidence in their achievements, increase their trust in others and develop strong inter- personal relationships.

The Oasis submission was put to the DES but the initial response was disappointing. HMI argued that the proposals relating to both primary and secondary schools trespassed on the responsibilities of the

LEAs concerned and, because of the rules of government accounting, could not qualify for central government funding. In the light of this setback, Oasis recast the proposal to concentrate on the 13-19 year group for whom the youth services had responsibility- essentially older pupils in secondary school. This time the bid was successful and in September 1996 Arthur Brown joined Oasis to manage the Trust's 'Excluded Pupils Project' which was soon to be renamed 'Fresh Start'. The first task of the new unit was to approach local schools and bring together young people to act as mentors and group leaders. Members of the UK Frontline Teams working in London, and students on the Youth Ministry Course, (see chapter 6) provided an initial pool of volunteers, but the pressure on their own training needs necessarily imposed limits on the time they could offer. It was clear that additional staff would need to be recruited if a proper service was to be provided to the schools and, more importantly, the pupils themselves.

Soundings were made of local schools and the Alwyn Girls' School in Bermondsey, the Warwick Park School in Peckham, and the Pupil Referral Unit, also in Peckham, all inner city Schools, welcomed the help that Oasis was offering. A management committee was set up to oversee and evaluate the work in the schools, with representatives from the schools themselves, educationalists and Oasis management all playing a part.

The early days of the project were extremely challenging as inexperienced young people sought to develop relationships with pupils, many of whom had little interest in learning or respect for their teachers and classmates. The teachers themselves were relieved to be able to pass over these youngsters to others, at least for a short time: the young people, for their part, reacted positively to those who did not in their eyes represent the 'educational establishment'.

One of the first tasks of the new mentors was to establish ground rules for conduct in the context of group lessons. The aim was to persuade the pupils to 'own' the rules to which the group would work. It was interesting to note, quite early on, that the pupils wanted to work to clear rules and were ready to punish those of their number who chose to break them. Thus the rules "No swearing, no insulting, no racial abuse, no gender discrimination, no bullying etc." and many others were agreed. Quite severe penalties were thought by the pupils themselves to be appropriate for those who broke them.

At the individual level, project staff members, supplemented by members of Frontline Teams and the Youth Ministry Course, assisted pupils as needs arose and sought to gain pupils' trust and build positive relationships. This sometimes led to dealings with parents, teachers, local officials and police, both as mediators and advocates, as mentors sought to understand and support the pupils who were so close to falling out of mainstream education.

Evaluation by Oasis management and then, significantly, by HMI showed that the project was being run well and was beginning to make an impact on the lives of the pupils and their schools. It was, however, a process that would take many months, even years, and it was extremely resource intensive.

Two examples, one from Alwyn School and the other from Warwick Park, provide an indication of the results which in many cases were achieved. At Alwyn, Oasis worked initially with year 8 girls, a notorious year in many schools. One class in particular had a great deal of conflict within it. Oasis was asked to provide support to the class as a whole. Two members of staff, working with a volunteer were allocated to the task. They were able to interact with the groups and engage in certain activities, facilitating group sessions. They also ran a residential weekend for the class. During the weekend, girls who had been in serious conflict began to know each other better, to work together and, by the end of the weekend, were able to say positive things about each other. Some of the conflict related to issues of race and overall there was a greater degree of unity established than had existed before.

In Warwick Park, Arthur Brown and Tim Shinde, (who had come from India and was studying on the Youth Ministry course) were asked by the Children's Society and the year Head to work with three year 8 boys. All were of African-Caribbean origin. One had already been temporarily excluded on a number of occasions and had been in and out of school and involved in a number of conflicts with staff. The other two were disruptive in class and rude to their teachers. All had been involved in fighting with their peers. The team met with them once a week for about an hour and a half. The sessions included some games/ice-breakers, which helped them to relax, and team-building activities were employed to improve their ability to communicate and work together constructively. The team also offered the pupils the opportunity to talk about their experiences of life, their frustrations and their hopes for the future. Role plays/drama, which explored various ways of dealing with conflict, were also used regularly.

In October 1999, Arthur Brown left the project to become a full-time mentor at the Geoffrey Chaucer Comprehensive School in Central London. The school had recently received Oasis mentors for the first time, bringing the number of schools benefiting from the project to four. However, despite the continuing grant from the DfES and another from the Bridge House Trust, the scope for extending the project was limited. The Government grant could not be used to help pupils below the age of thirteen even though problems were becoming increasingly apparent in primary schools. It became clear that in order to extend the scope of the project to include more schools, including primary schools, and increase the age range of the pupils served, another source of funding was required.

The answer was found through agreements with individual LEAs who were now putting significant resources into tackling the problems of exclusion. By 2002, a significant number of contracts were signed whereby Oasis provided its now specialised mentoring services to LEAs in return for a fee. An important new development occurred when an agreement was reached with Southwark LEA to assist pupils in the transition from primary to secondary education. This programme supported pupils in year six, with mentors attempting to establish their hopes, fears and aspirations in respect of their transition to the next phase. Mentors also assisted with practical matters and maintained their support for the pupils concerned during their early months in secondary school. The value of this lay in the fact that the primary school years and the successful transition to the secondary phase are recognised as key factors determining future educational achievement.

A further development was the first appointment of an Oasis worker to the West Northfield Safer Communities project in Birmingham. The introduction was made by the Deputy Chief Constable of the West Midlands Police, and the worker concerned worked in partnership with a range of organisations, including the LEA and the police. This represented the first extension of the project outside London.

Oasis also became one of the first members to the National Mentoring Network funded by the Department for Education Skills (DfES). This offered a kite mark to organisations that met acceptable standards of performance, and Oasis was one of the first to receive this recognition.

By 2004 lessons were being provided in 30-35 schools in the London Boroughs of Southwark, Lambeth and Bexley, as well as in Birmingham. All the pupils involved had been referred to Oasis by the schools concerned. Fifty per cent of the schools were engaged in the Primary Transition Project and all the pupils were on the margins of exclusion. The DfES continued to provide a grant to assist the older pupils.

The extension of Oasis activities into so many schools, and the wide range of services which were offered, provided a model of the way that churches and other Christian organisations could contribute effectively to the communities in which they lived. With the Faithworks project encouraging the involvement of Christians in the life of their communities, Youth Inclusion, as the project was now called, offered a template for mentoring work in schools across the country.

But even more important in terms of Steve Chalke's original vision, Oasis was establishing itself as a credible organisation in the educational world. Meetings were held with officials in No 10 Downing Street in 1998, and discussions about a possible City Academy were held with the London Borough of Southwark in 2000, but these came to nought. The outcome of the discussions with Southwark came as a keen disappointment. The LEA was faced with a choice between a school run in association with Oasis, and one run with the City of London. To all appearances the greater resources of the City and the fact that Oasis was a Christian organisation, were decisive. Oasis was, however, committed to another attempt to achieve its long held objective of running a school with Christian values within the State Sector. Soundings were taken of LEAs and it was the London Borough of Enfield which responded most positively. The gates were now open.

Thus in Spring 2004 Oasis was included in a list of organisations who would be given a grant by the Government to finance a feasibility study for a City Academy, specialising in business and enterprise, and located in Enfield. The consultation document made it clear that the admissions policy of the Oasis Academy Enfield would be totally inclusive, i.e. it would accept students irrespective of ability or faith;

those with disabilities or learning difficulties would also be eligible. When fully operational it would provide 1150 places, starting in 2007 with year 7 (age 11) alongside a sixth form entry "in order to give new pupils older role models".

The governing body of the Academy would consist of representatives from the DfES, the LB of Enfield, Oasis Trust, parents and staff governors and others from the community appointed for their skills and expertise.

The consultation document made clear that as Oasis Trust was a Christian foundation, the Academy's ethos would be rooted in Christian core values, which it was hoped would permeate every aspect of the school's life. These included "valuing everyone and protecting individual rights to freedom and choice, working against discrimination and social exclusion, and respecting the beliefs and practices of other faiths". More than that, the vision was for a school that would also provide a hub for the community with a wide range of facilities open to all, including sports facilities, a healthy living centre and youth activities.

Although by 2004 there was still some way to go before the Oasis school opened its doors, the vision was slowly becoming a reality. Looking further afield, schools of various kinds were being run by Oasis as far apart as Bangalore in India, Harare in Zimbabwe, Kampala in Uganda and São Paolo in Brazil.

By 2007, when the new school is expected to open its doors, it will have been twenty-one years since Oasis first met with Government to discuss the possibilities, and many more since Steve had his original vision. Visions may occur overnight, but working them out requires application, patience, but above all, faith.

Chapter 6
Training Leaders for the Present and the Future

Frontline Teams

In the first year after its formation in 1985, Oasis' work consisted largely of Steve's evangelistic activities and initial searches for a suitable site for a hostel. Steve travelled the length and breadth of the country speaking at missions, conferences, etc. but it soon became clear to him that he could not bring the Christian message to the young people of Britain entirely on his own. He increasingly realised that it was only as local churches took their responsibilities seriously, to reach out to others in their communities, that any impact would begin to be made. He was conscious that many churches in inner city London were struggling as members left to set up homes in the suburbs. Many churches had been in decline since the end of the Second World War. If the message of Jesus was to make a significant impact through those churches, something had to be done.

Steve decided that the best course of action was to appeal to young people to leave the comfort of their home churches and to volunteer for work in the Inner City. He asked a Minister friend, Paul Jackson, if he would be prepared to take a team into his church in Paddington. Westbourne Park Baptist Church had a large building but was poorly attended, and it had clearly seen better days. It was located close to one of London's main railway stations in an area notorious for its drugs and prostitution, but it had a leadership that was ready to innovate and take risks in the interests of reaching out to the many needy people around it.

With Paul's agreement, Oasis placed an advertisement in the Baptist Times asking young people to "join Steve Chalke on the front line". Thus, the name Frontline was born. Six applications were received and, following a 'selection' day when candidates were assessed for their suitability, the first team started work in September 1986. The results were immediate and immensely encouraging. Early in 1987 eleven people became Christians through the coffee bar, eight of whom were men. Seven people also recommitted their lives to Christ and were baptised. On one occasion a member of the Westbourne Park team found a woman at her back door about to jump from the sixteenth floor of a tower block. Happily, she was persuaded to come down and to address her problems in a different way.

In September 1987, some 21 young people joined the project and the work was expanded to six London churches (all Baptist): Westbourne Park, Underhill in Barnet, Battersea Chapel, Gipsy Road in West Norwood, Northcott Road in Clapham, and Clapham Baptist Church. In the following year the number of team members grew to 30. One of the teams was located at Haddon Hall Baptist Church in Tower Bridge Road, close to the centre of the capital. The church had been bombed in the war but now had comparatively new premises that were seriously underused. Although there were some 18 members on its books, the active membership was nearer 8. These were largely elderly people who faithfully continued to meet, worship and pray together. The fellowship was led by George Denton who, when approached by Oasis, readily agreed to accept a team and to give it accommodation in the church flat. Its task in the first year was to establish relationships and build up contacts in and around the church.

By early 1988 Oasis desperately needed more space for its offices and eventually summoned up courage to ask if it could have access to more space in Haddon Hall. Graciously, the church agreed and Oasis moved in before the start of the 1989-90 training year.

The Frontline project was advertised as "A full-time urban evangelism and church 'on the job' training programme". The course consisted of one day of training, with the rest of the week given over to work in the placement churches under the broad direction of the leadership of the churches concerned. The training days consisted of times of devotion, lectures and seminars on a range of subjects, including personal spiritual growth, theology and apologetics. It included applied teaching dealing with issues likely to arise in the churches in which team members were placed e.g. how to understand and confront the growing problem of drugs. Specialist speakers were brought in to deal with many of these issues. 'Frontliners', as they came to be known, were also required to engage in personal research projects relevant to their particular ministry. Time was also allotted each week to prayer and personal help and guidance. Projects included research into aspects of AIDS and its impact on the local community, and the leadership of underprivileged young people on Outward Bound courses, amongst many others.

Work in the churches included involvement in local schools, street evangelism, (sketch board evangelism was particularly popular), youth /children's work, home visiting, running coffee bars, pastoral care, helping to disciple new Christians, and leading worship. In most churches, the main emphasis was on evangelism and mission. Some teams were given teaching in Evangelism Explosion and similar techniques, but the main thrust was reaching out into the community in a variety of practical ways. Local house-to-house surveys were developed to ascertain local needs. At the end of 1987-88, it was recorded that the teams had knocked on some ten thousand doors. This helped the teams to establish an effective presence for their churches in their localities. Many new activities were also started and most of these continued when the teams left.

The Frontline experience was not, however, without its problems and frustrations. The young people involved had been carefully chosen at 'selection weekends' and references obtained from pastors and youth leaders. Team leaders were also carefully selected and were usually people who had been in secular employment, sometimes in well paid positions. But the majority of the team members were away from home for the first time, most were young and inexperienced, and the churches to which they were assigned had little experience of engaging four to six young people "on the staff". Many of the difficulties were predictable and possibly unavoidable. Some team members became homesick once they had been assigned to their church. Others had, at best, significant problems and, at worst, tragedies, at home to cope with. One or two even felt that they had made a mistake in joining Frontline, and wanted to go home. Generally, however, the drop-out rate was very low (even non-existent in some years) compared with other volunteer programmes.

Perhaps even more important were relationship issues within the teams, and between the teams and the churches in which they were working, some of whom were struggling to adapt to new ideas and different styles of worship. The most acute problems usually arose early in each calendar year when the first phase of excitement had worn off, and the teams were faced with the long cold months of January to March.

These issues presented the leadership of Frontline with formidable day-to-day pastoral and organisational challenges. The issues ranged from an acute shortage of beds to coping with illness and the need for the development of a strategic plan for each church. On one occasion a Frontline volunteer was arrested and imprisoned for a serious offence, and it was not unusual for churches or volunteers to withdraw at the last moment, just as a training year was about to begin. Nonetheless, under the leadership of Simon Crisp, and then Tim Mungeam, the first national coordinators, the project grew in strength and confidence and additional staff were taken on board. Both leaders had been Frontline volunteers and knew the difficulties and problems.

In 1989/90 Oasis was able to supply fifteen teams involving 57 young people to churches in London, including for the first time, an Anglican church. By now, the demand for teams from London and beyond was much greater than Oasis could hope to meet. Requests for teams came from places as far apart as Bristol in the South West, Birmingham in the Midlands and Newcastle in the North East. As a result, six further teams were placed in the North East and four in Birmingham.

The teams in the North were located in Newcastle (2), Sunderland, Consett, Crook and Middlesborough. It was clear that they would need local leadership even if their programmes followed broadly the same models as those now well established in London. Accordingly a North East Director, Steve Halliwell, was appointed to co-ordinate the teams and to develop Oasis work more widely in that part of the country. Steve had studied at Cliff College, spent a year with the Birmingham Inner City Mission and coordinated youth work in Sheffield. He was therefore well equipped for the task. The new Oasis office was set up in Sunderland where training was carried out on one day a week, as in London. Much of the support for teams in this part of the country came from Rev. Eric Westwood who gave great support and encouragement to the Oasis leadership as they took the major step of extending the work to the north-east of England.

Two ex-Frontline volunteers - Jim Kilpin and Juliet Walton, headed up the new work in Birmingham. They were known to be 'going out' together and the leadership recognised that putting them together in a leadership position outside London entailed some risk. If the relationship flourished, all well and good, but if not, how would the work be taken forward? Happily, the couple became engaged and the work proceeded strongly in four churches in the city. Juliet was also able to develop work amongst prostitutes close to where she lived. She and Jim like many others, went on to train at Spurgeon's and in due course the couple set up a church in Shadwell in east London.

The Baptist Union was very supportive of these developments, providing a grant of £40,000 for work in Birmingham and the North East, just when it was most needed.

The development of teams in Birmingham provided the opportunity to establish Oasis more widely in the West Midlands. With the help of the Christian organisation 'Cornerstone', an office was leased close to New Street railway station, and the administration of the Christmas Cracker project was moved from London. This relieved pressure on accommodation in Haddon Hall and created a core of activities in Britain's 'second city'.

The number of Frontline teams reached a peak in the early '90s with some 70 members. It might well have increased further but for two factors. First, they were proving a heavy drain on Oasis', often precarious, financial resources. The cost of running the teams was substantial, but the churches they were serving were in no position to contribute substantially for the help they were receiving. In 1989 there was a shortfall of £17,000 and although this was turned into a small surplus by 1995, the deficits in the early years, together with deficits on mission and the Christmas Unwrapped project, posed an enormous strain on the Trust's resources.

Second, Frontline Teams Abroad (see chapter 8) began to take off in the early 1990s. Oasis was faced for the first time with the problem of running programmes that appeared to compete with one another.

However, despite the attractions of living and working in exotic locations abroad, enough young people were found who were dedicated to helping in the inner cities of the UK. By 1995 some 500 young people had participated in the project, supplemented by a number from the Salvation Army who joined the programme as active partners.

The help given to the churches was considerable and the benefits to volunteers equally so. In the words of the Minister of Westbourne Park, "Coming on Oasis squeezes ten years of growth into one". Moreover, large numbers of Frontliners and their leaders moved on into various forms of ministry both within Oasis and with other Christian organisations. A significant number also became ministers after further training at Spurgeon's. Equally, if not more importantly, were the majority who went into secular employment of various kinds, better prepared for the challenges of being Christians in a sometimes hostile or indifferent environment. Oasis held the view, which it has maintained throughout its life, that there is or should be no distinction between the secular and the sacred, and that the whole of a person's life, wherever it is lived out, should be dedicated to the service of God.

Spurgeon's/Oasis Course in Church Planting and Evangelism

When the first Frontline team was set up in 1986, no one in Oasis dreamt that the idea would provide the first building block in a structure of training and development, enabling young people to move through Oasis to become ministers and Christian workers throughout the UK and abroad. One of the strengths of the organisation was its commitment to taking and moulding essentially very raw material through various stages of formal training and experience. This not only helped the individuals concerned, it also generated an organisational ethos - a particular approach to work in the Trust - which was positive, innovative and, perhaps above all, enthusiastic. Part of this was the natural exuberance of youth, part a deep belief in and commitment to the Christian message, especially its requirements for social justice, and part a reflection of the leadership of Steve Chalke and others.

The second building block in the structure was the Spurgeons/Oasis course in Church Planting and Evangelism, the story of which is set out below.

Having been trained at Spurgeons, Steve maintained his links with the College. He was aware of his debt to the College and was fully committed to it, but he also felt that his four years of training had not been entirely appropriate for the kind of work to which he now felt called. He also noted that some of his friends had dropped out of the ministry, and he began to think about the changes that might be made to enable the College better to equip its students for the modern world. The opportunity to express these thoughts occurred at a Baptist Union Assembly when the Rev. Paul Beasley-Murray, the College Principal, spoke about the need for the Baptist denomination to plant more churches. At the end of the address, Steve stated that he concurred with what had been said, but wondered what the College was planning to do about it. Paul Beasley-Murray responded by saying that there were no plans at present but he would like to explore what the possibilities might be. The Principal himself was keen to provide a Master's Degree on top of the other degrees on offer, but Steve was convinced that a completely new course was needed, offering training specifically focussing on church planting and evangelism.

Steve was subsequently elected to the College Council where further discussions took place. He also lectured, together with others, at a College evening class on the theology and practice of youth ministry and evangelism. Following further discussions within the College, and despite some question marks as to whether the proposed course would work in practice, the College agreed to go ahead, provided Oasis could find the £30-40,000 which was needed to get it up and running! A generous donor provided a large proportion of the money and the Faculty finally agreed in 1988 to introduce the course, to be jointly owned, and known as the 'Spurgeons with Oasis Course in Church Planting and Evangelism'. It recognised that there was an enormous disparity nationally between goals for church planting and the level and availability of the training provided.

There was still much work to be done on the syllabus and on the teaching arrangements. By the autumn, however, Oasis was able to announce publicly that, together with the College, it was launching a new course designed to catch the tide of church planting that many hoped would be a feature of the Decade of Evangelism planned for the final ten years of the 20th century. The Oasis Newsletter explained that the concept behind the course was to offer training specifically

71

designed for evangelistic/church planting ministries "within the context of an inner city environment." The theological and academic traditions of Spurgeons, combined with Oasis' experience of urban mission would, it was felt, provide a solid foundation for the course.

The curriculum, however, was quite different from anything that had been offered before. It would be in modular form and students would spend two days a week at the College. The rest of the week would be spent studying and working in placement churches. Didactic teaching would be combined with learning by doing, or 'praxis' as it is known in the educational and training world. Tony Campolo in the United States was a keen proponent of praxis and his thinking had influenced Oasis.

The vision was of an army of evangelists working in churches, itinerant ministries, and in church planting situations, equipped with the necessary skills and underpinned by biblical and theological understanding. For the first time, students applying to the College would have the opportunity to choose whether to specialise in the traditional training courses for Pastoral ministry or to concentrate on evangelism and its associated requirements. Hearing of the course, the evangelist Billy Graham was quoted as saying, "This unique Spurgeon's/Oasis initiative marks a new era for evangelism in Britain".

The plan was to start with six students in 1989 and to increase the intake to twenty in 1990, although the College felt that eight new students in the second year might be more realistic. A joint Steering Committee was set up to oversee the running of the course and its development, and to resolve any such issues which might arise between the two organisations.

The post of Director of Studies was advertised in the normal way and the Rev Stuart Christine was appointed jointly by the College and Oasis in 1989.

At the time of his application, Stuart was the tutor in New Testament theology at the College. Previously he had spent eleven years with the BMS World Mission engaged in church planting in Brazil. He immediately set about writing the curriculum for the Diploma of Mission Studies. His theological understanding, commitment to evangelism, and experience of church planting made him ideally equipped to start and establish the new course. This would initially offer the Cambridge Diploma of Theology awarded by the CNAA, and a Diploma of Mission Studies awarded by the College. It would be tutored and taught by staff at the College supplemented by visiting lecturers.

The introduction of the new course into the College's training programmes posed formidable challenges for the College and Oasis, as well as for the students and the churches concerned. For the College, the course meant the appearance of a group of students, on just two days a week, who had, for the most part, very different backgrounds from the residential College students preparing for pastoral ministry in the traditional Baptist mode. Some had come out of church or secular employment, some, but by no means all, lacked academic qualifications, and some had worked in tough inner city areas and were less middle class than the generality of students at the College. On the other hand, all the students had a burning desire to reach out to others with the Gospel, and motivation was unlikely to be a problem. In any case, Stuart's enthusiasm for mission was infectious and proved a powerful driving force to the new intake.

There were also risks for the College as it moved away from some of its well-established criteria governing student selection. Charles Spurgeon had held the view that students should be trained at the College by virtue of their ability to "win people for Christ". For a College committed to high academic standards, the arrival of students with markedly differing levels of academic qualifications and ability raised quite difficult issues around the delivery of the course and the assessment of the candidates. The placement churches were also challenged as they sought to accommodate students, many of whom were raw and inexperienced in ministry.

The structure of the course, the character of the students, and the fact that they were often based in churches some distance away from the College, meant that full integration was unlikely to be easy, certainly in the first few years. So it proved to be. Being in a minority, they stood out as a group. Equally, it had been hoped that the students would play an integral part in the mission life of Oasis, but this too proved difficult to achieve.

Nonetheless, by academic year 1991-92 the course had reached its full complement of thirty - a significant proportion of Spurgeon's intake. This occurred at a time when the Baptist Union was raising questions about the demand for Baptist ministers and Baptist colleges were under financial pressure as a result of the shortage of candidates. The new course offset this to some extent. As it became established it became part of the wider movement across the country, helping to give church planting a higher profile, and putting it back on the agenda of some churches.

The course now offered three options. The 3-year course was designed mainly for people called into full-time ministry. In addition to the two days spent at the College, students spent their time in practical training, home study and further training leading to other qualifications such as a BD or Diploma in Theology. This course became a recognised route towards the Baptist ministry and as such introduced a major change in the denomination's thinking about its ministerial recognition arrangements.

The other two courses were the Certificate in Church Planting and Evangelism, involving one day a week in College for two years; and the Award in Church Planting and Evangelism, involving one day a week in College for one year. The aim for all the courses was to offer an integrated approach to learning, with theological, missiological, ecclesiological and sociological elements combined throughout.

In 1992 Stuart Christine returned to Brazil as a BMS missionary, having successfully developed the curriculum and launched the course. He had written the book "Planting Tomorrow's Churches Today"[1] in partnership with Rev. Dr. Martin Robinson, and was a leading figure in the church planting movement. Whilst in Brazil he continued to put theory into practice, planting churches in the Favelas, or slums, of São Paulo. After several years he was again to work with Oasis as he accepted Frontline Teams and led a new organisation, ABIAH, which was engaged in setting up and running pre-schools and planting churches. In time ABIAH was to become Oasis Brazil and Stuart became a member of the International Council. (See chapter 8 "Into all the World"). He was succeeded at Spurgeon's by Dr Stuart Murray, an expert in urban mission, well able to move the course forward.

For Oasis, the course was the realisation of what it believed to be essential for the growth of the church in the United Kingdom. Nonetheless, it struggled with the ongoing financial cost, and both

[1] Published by Monarch Publications

Spurgeon's and Oasis, with the best will in the world, found it less than easy to operate the course under joint ownership. It proved hard to apportion financial costs and people were confused by the joint ownership messages coming from the two institutions. It was very helpful therefore that, at the inception of the course, Oasis and the College had agreed to review its progress after five years.

Senior members of the College, including the Principal, working with senior members of Oasis, consulted widely whilst examining the course's objectives and operation in some detail. The review concluded that the objectives of the course had been achieved and, amongst other recommendations addressing the difficulties outlined above, proposed its extension to other parts of the UK. Most important of all the review concluded that it was achieving what it called its 'Kingdom Aims'.

Youth Ministry Course

During the Mission Team's tours of the country, and with the benefit of information supplied to Oasis by the Frontline Teams, it became clear that there was a shortage of appropriately trained youth leaders in the UK, right across the denominations. Although the YMCA's George Williams College had been training youth leaders with reference to Christian spirituality for some years, this was the exception rather than the rule. Youth groups, in the main, were being led either by ministers trained in theology with little or no training in youth work, or by youth leaders who had been trained in youth and community work who had only a layman's understanding of the Bible or knowledge of theology.

When Peter Staley joined Oasis to run Christmas Unwrapped and other special projects, he brought to the Trust knowledge and experience of a training initiative called ' Brainstormers'. This had for some years made a valuable contribution to youth leadership training, with weekend youth conferences attracting an increasingly large number of youth leaders and workers. An event held at Brean Sands in 1989, run by Youth for Christ, Elm House Christian Communications Limited and Oasis, had attracted some 1500 youth leaders and had indicated the appetite for training that existed up and down the country. Valuable as Brainstormers was, however, it could not of itself meet the demand for training in depth.

In response to this, Simon Parish, who at the time was heading up mission, and Heather Evans, who had joined Oasis and was running Capital Radiate (see next section) felt that something needed to be done. They spoke to Andy Matheson who had recently started as Director of Training while on a two-year sabbatical from India. Andy then worked on designing a course that combined theological training, youth and community input and leadership skills. In 1991 the decision was taken by the leadership to launch the course. As a graduate of Avery Hill Teacher Training College (now Greenwich University) Andy sought the cooperation of the college in teaching the youth and community work component, and he entered into discussions with Spurgeon's College about the provision of the theological element, represented by the Cambridge Diploma of Theology. Supplementing these formal courses were lectures and seminars by experienced youth workers touching on a wide range of aspects of church-based youth ministry, leading to the Oasis Certificate in Youth Ministry.

Following the 'praxis' model which was now being used successfully in the training of the Frontline Teams, and which was integral to the Spurgeon's course in Church Planting and Evangelism, the new course required students to spend three days each week in a church placement in London, enabling them to put their formal training into practice as they tackled all the issues and problems which youth workers faced in their churches and youth organisations, week in and week out.

The course began in September 1991 with an initial intake of thirteen students committed to two years of study. In the following year the number of students rose to thirty and enquiries suggested that there would be a further increase in 1993-94. The demand from churches for students exceeded the supply, and churches were now being placed on a waiting list. Meanwhile, steps were being taken to ensure academic credibility and Spurgeon's College played a major role in enabling the course to gain recognition to enable successful candidates to receive a Certificate of Higher Education from the University of Wales.

Oasis training, now with some 250 trainees overall and rising, was becoming a significant feature in its increasing number of activities. This was a reaction to the perceived needs of the churches in the UK, but it was also part of a conscious decision by the leadership to develop programmes which would provide increased financial stability through the generation of predictable income flows. Neither its social care programmes nor its mission activities could offer this. For the Youth Ministry Course financial viability meant not merely an expansion in numbers but the difficult decision to run the Cambridge Diploma of Theology within Oasis rather than at the College, thus saving £18,000 per year.

But other changes were also required to consolidate what had been achieved and to prepare the way for further expansion. The teaching of the Youth and Community component was switched from Avery Hill, which was proving too expensive, to training in house under a tutor from the YMCA. This enabled the course to offer the YMCA Certificate in Youth Work. Furthermore, the Baptist Union agreed in principle to the accreditation of youth workers and evangelists, an important development bearing on the career progression of young people graduating from the course. There were also a number of staff changes. Mark Vernon, an experienced youth leader from St. Mark's Church, Yately, was appointed to run the course in 1992 and the Rev. Peter Swaffield, a Baptist minister, was approached about the possibility of teaching the Cambridge Diploma in Haddon Hall as Head of the Training Department.

By the middle of the decade, plans were taking shape for a second teaching centre in the North of England. Mark Vernon entered into discussions with the Nazarene Theological College and the course was introduced and validated by the University of Manchester in 1996, and then extended to Glasgow Bible College, (now the International Christian College).

However, one vital element was still missing, namely recognition by the youth and community profession through endorsement by the National Youth Agency and recognition by the Joint Negotiating Committee (JNC) as conferring professional status. Efforts were made over the years to raise the qualification to a Diploma of Higher Education and to obtain the necessary status in the training world. Perhaps the most important decision bearing on this, taken by Oasis soon after its course had started, was not to join in the development of a degree course in cooperation with the Centre for Youth Ministry, a consortium comprising Oxford Youth Works, Frontier Youth Trust, Youth for Christ, St John's College Nottingham, Ridley Hall Cambridge and the Bristol Baptist College. The leadership was reluctant to join the consortium because the Oasis course was already well advanced and it was reluctant to entertain the possibility of delay. Oasis felt moreover that the demand for training was such as to justify a number of such courses. Whilst Oasis had led the way, it welcomed the further provision of the training facilities so badly needed across the country.

Initially, the decision appeared to have been unwise. The Centre for Youth Ministry developed an Honours course at B.A. level, obtaining full professional recognition. This continued to elude Oasis and after repeated efforts to gain recognition, the decision was taken to rewrite the course from scratch. Happily, this proved a success and the Youth Work and Ministry course (as it was renamed), was accredited to degree level by the University of Wales and validated by the Welsh Youth Agency in the academic year 2001-2002. Professional endorsement by the National Youth Agency of England, and its equivalent in Scotland was obtained in 2003. Moreover, in 2004 a new delivery centre was opened in Leeds.

Capital Radiate

A sense of anxiety about the amount and quality of youth work in the Churches was present in all the main denominations during the 1980's. The marked decline in young people attending church since the 1950's weakened the present day Church and the Church of the future. The Baptist denomination responded by asking all their area associations throughout the country to review the youth work in their churches. For the most part the results were very discouraging. In London, the situation alarmed the General Secretary of the London Baptist Association, Rev. Peter Wortley, and also Rev. Douglas McBain, who was about to become the Association's Superintendent.

Steve and his fledgling Trust were, of course, well known to both men and discussions took place as to what, if anything, Oasis could do to help the Association to address the matter. To its credit, the LBA was prepared to put money where its mouth was, and to make a grant to the Trust to employ a worker dedicated to the renewal of youth work in the capital. The letter offering the grant arrived in Oasis just two days after Steve believed he had found the right person, Heather Evans, for the task. Heather had been working with the Ambush Theatre Company, a

Chapter 7
Wider Horizons: Christmas Cracker

Up until 1989, Steve's focus, and that of Oasis more generally, had been on the development of work in London and, increasingly, other parts of the UK. However, the end of 1988 saw the beginning of a process of change as a result of a remarkable series of events, culminating in the first Christmas Cracker project in December 1989.

The project had its roots in the 'Beggars Banquet' run by the young people of Tonbridge Baptist Church in 1984, when money was raised for the developing world through an 'Eat Less, Pay More' restaurant on Tonbridge High Street. Cracker was to develop into one of the most remarkable national youth projects of its time because of its dynamic and innovative qualities and because, looking back, it is clear that it was seminal to the development of Oasis work in many countries of the world in future years. The story of how this came about rests largely on the meeting of three people whose combined experience, gifting and energies provided the catalyst for events, the impact of which are still being felt to this day.

Christmas Cracker - Early Days

Steve Chalke visited India for the first time in September 1988. He did so at the suggestion of Andy Matheson who was a teacher at Woodstock School in North India and who felt it would be good if Steve had an opportunity to see the world beyond the confines of the UK. Steve took up the suggestion without hesitation. Only a few months earlier George Verwer, the founder of OM, had said to him, "If your vision is UK sized, it is not like God's vision. He loves the world. Unless you are global, your work will be deficient"

Steve travelled to Woodstock in the north and Madras in the south (where his father had lived), passing through Delhi and Bombay. He was shocked and appalled by the poverty and deprivation that he saw and he vowed, on his return to Britain, to do something about it.

During his time in Bombay, Steve had an unpleasant stomach upset, like many first time visitors to India before and since. In an article in the Oasis newsletter 'Backchat' in November 1988, he wrote about how wretched he felt during his illness, but added:

"I was ill, but to be honest the real crisis was that I had been faced with a problem so huge, far reaching and complex that my brain couldn't even begin to take in its dimensions, let alone get anything near finding the answer. On the other hand I could not believe that God had taken me all the way out to India to allow me to return home and ignore the whole experience - this would have been a rather strange and meaningless waste of His resources."

In response, Steve produced a four-point plan, designed to support the work of the churches in Bombay. These included, crucially, the aim of "setting up a national youth project to help to finance and to assist the Church in programmes of setting up schools amongst the slums of Bombay, Calcutta and other cities, as well as to inspire the young people of Great Britain with a worldwide mission vision." Andy Matheson's suggestion had had the desired effect.

During his visit to Bombay, Steve met the Rev Viju Abraham, founder of the Bombay Urban Fellowship and pastor of a local church. Pastor Viju told his brother, Raju, now living in the UK, that he had met a young English pastor with a burning desire to bring the gospel to the teeming millions of people living in poverty in Bombay and other Indian conurbations. Raju was a consultant neuro-physician at Charing Cross Hospital in London and a person of great energy, imagination and initiative. He too had a deep yearning to help the country of his birth.

Hearing of Steve's determination to help the poor of India, Raju decided to arrange a meeting between Steve and another recent visitor to India who had also returned profoundly shocked by what he had experienced. His name was Balram (Ram) Gidoomal. Ram's family had been forced out of Pakistan at the time of partition in 1946, and had settled in Kenya where they had built up a prosperous business. However, following Kenya's Independence, Ram and his family had become refugees for a second time when they were deported in 1967 to the UK. There they established a home and a family newsagent business in Shepherd's Bush.

After the early days of hardship in London, Ram went to University and, having graduated with a degree in Physics and with a Research Fellowship in Management Science, began to make his own way in the world. Now a successful businessman and the UK Group Chief Executive of Inlaks, a multi-national company, Ram too had been profoundly affected by a visit to India on a business mission in April 1988. He recounts in his book 'Sari 'n' Chips':[1]

"I was absolutely devastated by the appalling sights I saw. I couldn't believe it. The pastors told me about the so called 'slum lords'. Imagine having to pay rent to live in a slum! I saw child prostitutes and five year olds - one of whom reminded me of my son - who did not even have a pavement to sleep on". He went on, "During the plane journey back in my first class lounge I broke down. I just could not take the caviar and champagne that was being offered on the plane. How could I be a Christian in such conspicuous luxury doing nothing about what I had seen? Could I co-exist on the planet allowing a group of human beings to live in the way I had just witnessed while doing nothing about it? I was faced with a choice of personal futures and I knew what I had to do."

Earlier, Ram had become a Christian from Hinduism when studying at Imperial College London. Whilst making his way in the business world, he began increasingly to feel that God might be calling him to Christian service. In 1985, he applied to an advertisement in the Christian magazine '21 CC'. On application, Ram was told that the company 'Christian Headhunters' were looking for someone at least aged fifty, which ruled 35 year old Ram out of the running immediately. Nonetheless, it was as a result of this application that he came to meet Raju Abraham, and Raju, for his part, saw Ram as someone of enormous potential.

[1] Published by MARC and South Asian Concern, 1993

A meeting was duly arranged to take place in Ram's Inlaks office at 23 Chesham Street, Belgravia, late in 1988. After sharing their recent experiences in India, Steve told Ram about the way in which his youth group in Tonbridge had raised money in 1984 to provide water wells in India, and that he thought the project 'Beggars Banquet' had the potential to be run by churches nationwide. Moving quickly into business mode, Ram asked Steve if he had a business plan for him to consider. Steve had just about heard of such things but had never prepared one! He nonetheless had the temerity to ask Ram for financial help to enable him to run similar projects in churches up and down the country. Ram agreed to do this provided the name 'Beggars Banquet' was dropped because of its ambiguity, and provided Oasis ran the project as a franchise, much like McDonalds.

Steve accepted the name change and, for his part, undertook to get some two hundred youth groups on board, each running an 'Eat Less, Pay More' restaurant. Ram figured that if two hundred groups could raise £5000 each, the result would be £1,000,000 for the developing world. He concluded that if he could help raise the administrative expenses associated with the project, all the money raised by the youth groups could go directly to meet the needs of the poor.

The first basic principle underlying the success of the project was now established. Ram would organise sponsorship and help raise administrative costs, Steve would generate ideas and run the project, and Raju would use his networks to ensure that the money raised, if possible in its entirety, would be used to best effect in South Asia and other parts of the world.

The planning now began in earnest for a nationwide project to take place around Christmas 1989. But first, it urgently needed early promotion; and second, it needed a new name to replace 'Beggars Banquet'.

The key factor in the early promotion of the project was the involvement of Hilary Saunders, the editor of '21 CC'. Hilary was present at the early meetings of the 'Troica' and gave Steve the opportunity to write about the project on a regular basis and so reach youth leaders and churches throughout the country. Although the magazine went through various changes of name over time, it played an integral part in the success of the project. Every effort was made to give the publicity a Third World feel, and Paul Clowney, a professional from a well-known firm of graphic designers, offered his services. The result was a remarkable set of Neo Zulu graphics - a design that somehow represented simultaneously the cultures of Africa, India and South America.

'21 CC' (later to become 'Alpha') was also closely linked to Spring Harvest, the large Christian convention held around Easter in different parts of the country. It was decided that the Easter 1989 Spring Harvest would be the ideal launching pad for the project to be run later that year.

A decision also had to be taken on the name. Early in 1989, at a meeting in the new Oasis offices in Haddon Hall Baptist Church, the name of 'Christmas Cracker' was agreed. The precise origin of the name is still uncertain, but it was probably derived from a group of young people at the church who had been asked to come up with ideas that would attract young people and gain media attention. Their response was ingenious and striking. They wanted to construct the largest Christmas cracker in the world and in doing so to find a place in the Guinness Book of World Records. The name also lay comfortably with '21 CC'!

The structure of the project was now taking shape and expectations were high that something really significant in the Christian world was about to emerge. The key involvement of people such as Ram and Raju, who were outside Oasis (though Ram later became a trustee), and the expected scale of operations was such that it was decided to set up a separate Charitable Trust under the name 'Christmas Cracker'. The first trustees were Ram Gidoomal (Chairman), Raju Abraham, David Evans, Hilary Saunders and Steve Chalke. Graham Mungeam (then the new Executive Director of Oasis) was made Secretary and Rev. Gordon O'Neill was appointed Project Director.

When the group met early in 1989 to consider how to get 'Christmas Cracker' underway, they were immediately faced with financial challenges. Money was needed for a publicity video featuring Steve on location in India, and several thousand pounds were needed to produce the largest Christmas cracker in the world and to launch the project. Here Ram's business experience again became crucial. Following his strategy of 'pray and ask', he was able to persuade the Regional Director of Air India to provide free air tickets for the video filming. Further, he offered McGills Seafood Limited the opportunity to sponsor the event as a means of promoting the name of the company cost effectively, and they agreed. Further sums were, however, needed to cover all the other administrative costs. These were raised from Interserve by way of a loan and the part-time secondment to 'Christmas Cracker' of a staff member to help with publicity, and from Tear Fund who gave £5,000 on the understanding that they would have a significant role in the distribution of the money raised (along with the other donors).

Initially, the evangelical community were quite hesitant about getting involved, but Ram insisted that if Christian organisations would not support these initiatives to bring people out of poverty, he would go to the Hindu, Moslem and Sikh communities, many of whom subsequently gave significant gifts in support of the project.

There was one further piece of the jigsaw that needed to be put in place whilst the project was getting underway in the churches. When the money was successfully raised, how and to whom should it be distributed? What criteria would govern the difficult choices to be made between the many worthwhile organisations likely to apply?

To consider this vital question, Raju Abraham invited Steven Rand of Tear Fund, and Robin Thomson, a missionary theologian who had lived in India for 25 years, to join him in producing criteria that could be put to the Trustees. It was decided that no project should receive more than £20,000. This was to bring about what Raju called the 'mosquito effect', namely, helping a large number of small ministries, run by the nationals of the countries receiving funds, most of whom could not expect to raise funds from larger agencies. Second, all applicants would need to show that they were engaged in holistic mission. Third, in order to minimise risk, all applicants were to show that their work was well established and continuing.

Robin Thomson also undertook to write a mission manual as a resource for youth groups participating in the project, and as a module for the curriculum at St. John's College, Nottingham. Thus, another principle was now established.

Aims

'Beggars' Banquet', the pilot project run in Tonbridge in 1984, had had two principal aims - to encourage and enthuse the young people of the church and, in so doing, to raise funds for the developing world. These also became the core aims of 'Christmas Cracker', but following the appointment of Richard Wood, he and the Trustees began to shape it into something that was wider in scope and more complex in operation. The 1992 Annual Report stated that the project's aims were to:

- motivate young people to give their time and energy to work for others

- provide a project worthy of their energy and enthusiasm

- enable young people in church youth groups to work cooperatively amongst themselves and with other groups

- enable Churches and Christian organisations to work together with other sectors of the community

- teach young people work and life skills including those of business, organisation, management, marketing, accountancy, engineering and communication

- educate and inform young people about the needs and problems of the developing world

- provide resources for developing countries and the world's poor.

These aims reflected the developing thrust of Oasis in its mission activities in that there was a strong emphasis on inter-church co-operation and the involvement of the wider community. They also reflected the growing awareness, in educational and training circles, that young people needed to be properly prepared for the world of work and to develop life skills. These were still unfashionable and relatively minor aspects of the curriculum in most schools. However, the high levels of unemployment, particularly youth unemployment, in the recession of the early '90s were forcing the educational establishment to address the issues anew.

Principles

To meet these aims, all the projects over the eight years of the Trust's active life had the following characteristics:

- All projects were run by registered church groups individually, or more usually collectively (however, it is known that some unofficial projects were also run thus avoiding the registration fee)
- Projects were usually run for two years - the first as a pilot
- Every new project had to be modern, relevant, innovative and "funky", and so appeal to young people.
- Each year extensive resource backup was provided, including
  - A challenging and motivating video filmed at a relevant location in the developing world
  - A Christmas Cracker book advising how to set up new projects
  - A mission manual and other material on the world's needs
  - A continuous supply of tailor-made information, including a magazine "Cracking Up - The Mouth of Cracker"
  - An extensive programme of publicity involving local and national media and a strong 'brand image'
  - The involvement of celebrities from the world of politics, from TV, radio and entertainment, e.g. Government ministers, Simon Mayo of BBC Radio 1, Trevor McDonald the newscaster, the cast of East Enders and GMTV's Mr Motivator
  - Sponsorship from nationally known companies and organisations e.g. BT, Prontoprint, TNT Express and Sightsavers International
  - Training days

Furthermore, each project had to have:
- Strong and effective financial management and control
- Accountability and annual reports at the end of each year with the publication of results
- Post-project evaluation in the UK and for Cracker grants in-country, (to the extent that this was possible).

Additional Fundraising Events

All these characteristics were to be found in the annual Christmas initiatives run from 1989 up to and including 1996. They were supplemented by a number of special fundraising initiatives including 'Streets Apart', the youth dimension of the Oasis evangelistic initiative 'On Fire' (see chapter 3),

Other special fundraising events were held in conjunction with the new breakfast TV station, GMTV. In December 1993, an appeal was made on behalf of homeless people and in April 1994 GMTV was instrumental in raising £517,000 for the victims of the Latur earthquake in Western India. The appeal was made on television from a studio operating high up in the BT tower in Central London, manned by Oasis and Cracker staff. Cracker also put on a carol concert in support of the NSPCC. All these events gave Steve Chalke media exposure and provided valuable experience as he developed his interest in the media.

Details of each year's projects and a summary of financial results can be found in Appendix B.

Some Major Issues

It was unrealistic to expect a project as ambitious and as inventive as Christmas Cracker to run its course without major problems. By the mid 1990s, Christmas Cracker was established as a leading national charity working with youth and the developing world. It was unique among Christian organisations within the UK and countries in different parts of the world were adopting its ideas. Nonetheless, with the passage of time, problems began to emerge, the first from a totally unexpected source.

Christmas Cracker Versus Camelot

In the autumn of 1995, a member of staff in the Oasis office in London decided to have a Mars bar with his usual cup of coffee. On entering the nearest newsagent he saw a lottery scratch card named 'Christmas Cracker' and graphics which were virtually indistinguishable from those used by the Christmas Cracker Trust.

The secretary of the Trust, on receiving the information, informed the Chairman and immediately solicitors were instructed to argue that Camelot's action in selling such scratch cards constituted 'passing off'. They sought an undertaking from the company that they and their agents would cease selling the offending cards, withdraw all publicity relating to such products, instruct all retail outlets to cease selling the products, and to issue a public statement for publication in the media that the company's product had no connection with the Christmas Cracker Trust.

The association of the lottery with Christmas Cracker in the eyes of the public could hardly have been more serious for the Trust or for Oasis. On the lottery's inception, Steve Chalke and others had come out publicly against the principles and practice of the lottery. Moreover, the Trust's supporters and those directly involved in the project to date were known to share their views. There was therefore a threat to the supporter base of both charities and a serious risk that the public would believe that they were giving to Christmas Cracker when they bought the cards. Before long letters were being received from all parts of the country expressing concern.

There was, therefore, some consternation and disbelief that the reply from Camelot's solicitors did not in any way recognise or acknowledge the difficulties in which the Trust had been placed, nor the arguments which the Trust had put forward. In a nine-point submission the solicitors acting on behalf of Camelot sought to defend the company and concluded aggressively "Our clients have applied to register the name 'Christmas Cracker' as a service mark for lotteries".

Cracker's Trustees were not, however, minded to let the matter rest there, and on 24 October the Media office issued a press notice deploring the fact that Camelot had produced a scratch card with such scant regard for existing charitable work. It said, "By demonstrating a lack of sensitivity to the aims, reputation, and standing of a well-established youth charity, Camelot has succeeded in breeding confusion which threatens the continued success - even the very existence - of the 'Christmas Cracker' annual appeal".

In a further statement, Ram Gidoomal, the Trust's Chairman, pointed out that Camelot had launched the card when there was already much speculation in the press about "the damage the National Lottery is doing to the income of charities in general". He added, "It is particularly worrying that the Christmas Cracker Trust now faces the prospect of further damage".

By now the issue was in the public domain in both the local and the national press.

A further exchange of letters took place but with no apparent breakthrough. It was clear that if the matter were to be resolved at all, a face-to-face meeting between the parties would be necessary. At that point, with Cracker threatening to sue Camelot for the losses it was anticipating, and Camelot threatening to counter sue the Trust for many millions of pounds, a totally unexpected breakthrough occurred. Ram Gidoomal met a lawyer at a reception in the Mansion House and told him of the predicament in which the Trust found itself, with virtually no resources with which to take Camelot to court, but facing enormous and possibly fatal damage if it did not. The lawyer expressed his concern and offered to argue Cracker's case at the meeting with Camelot, which had by now been arranged.

At the meeting, Ram Gidoomal and the Trust's Secretary presented Camelot's Director of Communications and his team with clear evidence of "passing off" in the form of Cracker's publicity material set out alongside a range of scratch cards obtained from a local newsagent. Cracker's case was cogently argued and by the middle of November an amicable settlement was reached. Camelot agreed to state publicly that there was no connection between their latest instant game and the work of the Trust. They also agreed not to reprint the scratch card and not to use the name 'Christmas Cracker' for any future games. In addition, the company agreed to send leaflets to its 25,000 outlets throughout the UK, emphasising that no connection existed between the lottery and the charity, and asking them to inform customers accordingly. Finally, Camelot agreed an undisclosed payment to Christmas Cracker as a mark of goodwill.

In reporting the settlement the press represented the result as a triumph for the Trust. The headline in The Times, "Christian charity wins scratch card victory" represented the sentiments of other parts of the national and local press. Although the Trustees were gratified that the damaging conflict had been resolved in the Trust's favour, at a deeper level they were relieved that it appeared that no permanent damage had been done to its work. There were, however, other problems on the horizon.

Other Problems

After reaching a peak in 1992-93, there were signs of fatigue amongst the groups participating each year. Money continued to be raised through GMTV initiatives but the basic format involving church youth groups began to show signs of tailing off. Although some groups were continuing to operate strongly, others felt that they needed a rest from the extensive and onerous demands that had been made upon them year by year since 1989. However, the project was still meeting the non-monetary and less tangible aims that the trustees had agreed at the outset, including the better understanding of the challenges of the developing world and the enhancement of work and life skills. Moreover, the prospect emerged for the 1996 project to be run in conjunction with a charity with the reputation and standing of Sightsavers International. This offered the prospect of tackling the unfashionable but acute issue of preventable blindness in the developing world. Thus, the 1996 project began with renewed enthusiasm and high expectations on the part of the Cracker team.

Despite the efforts of all concerned (see appendix B) Christmas Cracker 1996 produced a disappointing result and a sum well short of the totals raised in previous years. In the light of this outcome, the Trustees decided to review the future of the Trust before finalising plans for a project in 1997.

The 1996 project had also been criticised by 'Youth Worker', the journal of the National Youth Agency. The Trustees, who regarded the attacks as inaccurate and unfair, held urgent meetings with the Agency who, after pressure, agreed to provide Cracker with the right of reply, which was duly taken up.

But with the passage of time it became clear that, rather than risk further decline, the project had run its course and should be brought to a close. A number of groups, most notably those in Ballymena in Northern Ireland, and in Rugby, nonetheless continued to operate for several years in view of the standing of Christmas Cracker projects in their respective locations.

Conclusion

Christmas Cracker came to an end on 31 January 1997. Ram Gidoomal explained the decision:

"Cracker has been a tremendous experience for us all. Whilst recognising that some (participants) will inevitably be disappointed, the Trustees feel that the time has come to bring down the curtain and to celebrate its achievements. Thousands have enjoyed taking part, thousands have been inspired to engage with the needs of the developing world, and thousands have been helped to take a step towards independence and out of poverty".

Cracker had provided a vehicle through which Christian youth groups were able to demonstrate their faith in very practical ways, challenging the Church and the general public alike to open their eyes to global poverty and its effects - to get involved and to make a difference. In the words of Cliff Richard, " I am excited by this original and creative idea: and don't let anyone say it's a shallow and emotional response to a few TV pictures. These young people are giving more than money, they've dug deeper in their pockets, they've given their time and energy to make the projects happen," and he was right.

In total over 1700 individual projects were run over eight years, plus well over 500 events. Over four million pounds were raised to support a range of aid and development activities right across the world, plus funds generated by GMTV and other supporting initiatives

But these figures represented only the tip of the iceberg. As a direct result of the projects, hundreds, even thousands of young people were motivated to give their lives to meeting the needs of the poor and disadvantaged. History was to show that Christmas Cracker, together with Oasis Frontline Teams, were key elements in the development of Oasis' work in India and in other parts of the world.

Christmas Cracker was followed by a number of other fund-raising projects, including one called 'The Big Take'. However, by the late 90's Oasis was switching its emphasis from raising money for the developing world, to direct involvement in the further development of Oasis bases abroad, as described in the next chapter.

Chapter 8
"Into all the World"

Historians say that it is difficult to determine the precise cause of any historical event or series of events. To the extent that it is possible to trace back the origins of Oasis work across the world, Steve Chalke's visit to India at Andy Matheson's invitation in 1988, leading to Christmas Cracker, must rank as the most proximate cause.

Following that visit, Steve told the Oasis trustees that he believed Oasis work should no longer be confined to the cities of the UK but extended to reach out to other cities around the world. The contacts established by Christmas Cracker provided the platform for this in a number of ways. The Cracker Trustees had always been aware of the project's potential, praying and believing that it could stimulate a new wave of interest in the developing world, especially amongst young people. They recognised that this would enhance the work of Oasis and similar organisations in the UK and elsewhere. So it proved to be.

Following the 1989 national project, groups from the UK were invited to India to see examples of the holistic ministries that Cracker was supporting. In 1990 one such group went to India for three weeks, followed by another group for 3 months later in the year. This gave the groups the opportunity not only to see the work but also to become directly involved. One member was John Nonhebel, a Cracker project leader from Ipswich, employed at the time by British Telecom. John became increasingly aware of a call to India and was destined to play an anchor role in that country in years to come.

By that time, Oasis 'Frontline Teams', as they were called, were well established in the UK. Andy Matheson, now working as Director of Training suggested that a similar model of ministry, offering support to local churches, combined with training for team members, had the potential to be equally effective abroad. He was given the go-ahead by the leadership to do a pilot project, choosing India as the location because that was where his experience lay. So was born the 'Frontline Teams Abroad' programme, or FTA as it came to be known.

The concept was simple but challenging. Teams would go abroad, at the invitation of local churches, to carry out whatever tasks the church leadership required. They would live as the people lived. Where practicable they would live with families in the homes of church members, sharing their food and working in the churches concerned. Their spending money would be limited, and they would not operate as UK tourists or Western businessmen, living apart in hotels or superior accommodation. (One team member in the early days even chose to live in a slum). Nor would they bring to local people the worst aspects of Western culture in terms of dress and social behaviour. They would be servants, not masters, cooperating with local pastors in whatever roles were thought to be most suitable.

For this ideal to work there had to be careful selection of group members and group leaders. Whilst particular skills, e.g., musical skills, were valuable and a bonus, the key criteria in those early days was a clear commitment to Christ, a willingness to serve, and ideally some early sense of a call to mission. Selection was held over two days when candidates were assessed against the above criteria, plus their ability to work in teams and flourish in an unfamiliar culture and environment.

After selection, and before the teams left for their destination, all the candidates went through health checks and 7 - 14 days training in cross-cultural mission. This proved to be of crucial importance because many group members joined the programme as very young Christians and some had spiritual and behavioural issues associated with their lives before becoming Christians, which needed to be addressed. The training also helped in the identification of leaders and welded the teams together. Following the initial training in the UK some further training was provided on their arrival in location.

Although the 'Cracker' visits to India had been for 3 weeks and 3 months, the latter was not felt to be long enough to enable the young people concerned to settle down and make a significant contribution. The first team went for a period of 8 months and thereafter experience showed that 6 months was the minimum required, offering a compromise between being too short a period to make an impact, and the need for team members to return home in time to prepare for higher education or for starting work. However, even 6 months sometimes seemed too short, as many team members felt that they had only just begun to drive on all cylinders when the time came to return home. On return, Oasis conducted a formal evaluation of their experience with a view to learning lessons for the benefit of their successors.

The pilot in India in 1991 had been a success and the following year another team went to Bombay and arrangements were made with the Mission Aviation Fellowship to receive teams in Tanzania. (Teams went to Tanzania for several years but it became clear that the requirements of the Mission did not sit comfortably with the Oasis model. They were discontinued by mutual consent when MAF set up its own programme specifically tailored to the mission's needs). However, it was not long before teams were going to several other countries and relationships developed that would eventually lead to the establishment of ongoing Oasis work.

India

By May 1992 a small group of young people had emerged who offered collectively the prospect of a 'permanent' Oasis presence in Bombay. Andy & Joan Matheson, who had a vision to work among the poor of the city, decided to base themselves there prior to their sabbatical in the UK. They needed to return to North India in order to renew their visa status but had been in contact with Viju Abraham who headed up an organisation in Bombay called Urban Ministry Centre. John Nonhebel was also thinking of returning after leading the first Frontline Team, and another member of that team, Ruth Cox, was expressing a similar interest. A meeting of all the parties took place and plans were laid for a small group of Oasis staff to be in Bombay by summer 1993 to establish ongoing work. Ruth Mustow, (now Cox) lead a second team to the city and then concentrated on developing

'Jacobs Well', a vision she had to empower marginalised women through vocational training; John Nonhebel initially concentrated on developing youth training initiatives for the churches, particularly those belonging to the Church of North India; whilst Andy Matheson headed up the base giving vision and leadership to develop the work on a whole range of fronts. They were supplemented by others over time, many returning to India following successful FTA experiences in different parts of the city. It was not long before the staff team grew to 20 which included some former FTA members, several secondments from Interserve and an increasing number of local Indian staff. Some of these were to be associated with Oasis for many years, taking senior positions. The Urban Ministry Centre under Viju Abraham's leadership provided a legal covering and gave Oasis great support and encouragement in the early years.

Meanwhile, Sam Rajshekhar, an Indian youth leader with 20 years experience with YFC, while studying in the UK, saw the BBC broadcast in 1992 about Steve's ministry as an evangelist. He subsequently enquired of Oasis in London as to whether he might join the Oasis team in India, whose mission, he observed, was very much in line with his own heart for the poor, particularly needy children. Sam met with Graham in London in April 1993 and then with Andy in Bombay in July of that year. Following some discussion about the wisdom of starting work in Bangalore, which was 600 miles from Bombay, so soon after the establishment of work there, Graham and Andy agreed that Oasis would go ahead and Sam was appointed to head up that base under Andy's oversight.

It was not long before teams from the UK and other countries were also going to Bangalore, and becoming engaged in local projects. The main emphasis initially was on care for 'rag pickers' in Sam's garage, and the provision of a day centre and community health care. Several small schools were also begun, offering high quality, mainly primary, education, and in 2001 schooling was provided for 100 child labourers under the National Child Labour Project. A large home and school for boys, 'Snehadhan' or 'A Friend's Gift', was also built on the outskirts of the city, large enough to hold the Oasis National Office and other facilities, including a vocational training unit. The building, which was opened in June 1999, aimed to provide a safe haven for boys who lived in dangerous or precarious situations, either on the streets or with abusive family members. Part of the schooling offered in both Bombay and Bangalore consisted of computer training under Oasis UK's 'Wire the World', now 'Net2work' programme.

Some of the activities, particularly youth activities, in Bangalore were run with the support and active co-operation of Young Life in America and World Servants from the Netherlands, who also made a helpful contribution to the construction of the Snehadhan School.

In Bombay, the initial thrust of the work consisted of several youth training initiatives in conjunction with the Church of North India, the Jacob's Well project giving training and employment to marginalised women, and an initiative to help street children on Kandivli railway station, part of the Bombay Metropolitan network. The latter project was run in cooperation with Apna Ghar, an Indian society, and involved a small home for boys and other forms of direct help.

This together with Frontline teams working in various churches in both Bombay and Bangalore formed the model for Oasis work over the next few years - support for the churches, training for youth leaders, training in employment for marginalised people, and care for children 'at risk'. Over time, further initiatives were to follow including medical work in a number of slums, 'Balwadis' for slum and street children of primary age, and the planning, building, and development of a home and care centre called 'Purnata Bhavan', or 'House of Wholeness', some 120 km outside Bombay. The plan was to provide a home, medical help and education for some 50 women and children affected by, or suffering from, HIV/AIDS.

Work also began in the north of the city amongst children living on the railway station at Thane, a major junction and terminus containing hundreds of children living rough. Initially Oasis opened a day centre and then in response to the pressing need, a night shelter for boys. Another project offered ministry to commercial sex workers in the Kennedy Bridge area of the city. Here a small and dedicated team of Indian workers sought to help those caught up in the extensive sex business of the city, encouraging and facilitating alternative lifestyles and introducing the gospel to the young women involved.

Simple Christian witness by word and action out of Christian love was a feature of all the projects. It was a great thrill for all the Oasis staff involved to see poor and marginalised children sharing in worship, learning to pray and coming to faith in a simple but life-changing way.

The rapid development of the work in India meant that appropriate managerial and legal structures needed to be put in place. In a crucial early development, UK trustees agreed that Oasis' work in India should be developed as an Indian legal entity, entirely separate from the UK. To that end, Andy Matheson worked with leaders in India, particularly Sam Rajshekhar, to set up Oasis India as a Society under Indian law. Potential trustees from Bombay and Bangalore met in Bangalore in February 1994 and the registration of the charity was formally approved in November of the same year. The Trustees who were all Indian, appointed Andy Matheson as Executive Director and Sam Rajshekhar as Assistant ED. The UK's Executive Director, Graham Mungeam, was also invited to be a member of the Committee of Management, to maintain strong ties with the UK. The thinking behind the setting up of Oasis India under indigenous ownership is discussed in Chapter 9.

Other important developments were the establishment of the Oasis Benevolent Foundation in 1998, a company registered under Section 25 of the Companies Act, to provide the legal framework for the manufacturing work of 'Jacob's Well', 'Paperworks', and 'Just Prospects', all projects designed to develop skills and give the prospects of employment to disadvantaged young people.

By 1995, Oasis India had offices operating in Bangalore and Bombay. In both centres there was a rapid increase in locally recruited staff and a high level of integration between UK and local personnel. However, there were signs that gaining effective integration between work in the two locations was going to prove a major challenge in the days ahead.

With the expansion of work across Bombay, the Oasis offices moved several times. Initially Oasis occupied a derelict site in Bandra, open to the elements and close to the police station. Later the team moved to a very small office without adequate headroom in Dadar, in central Bombay, where communications with other parts of the city were significantly easier. At the time of writing Oasis India is located in offices in Andheri East, close to the airport. These are leased from Asha Handicrafts, a Christian 'fair trade' organisation whose CEO, Lucas Caldeira was also a Trustee of Oasis India. Asha proved in this and many ways, to be particularly good friends to Oasis India over the years.

In such a huge city, the location of the office in Bombay was crucial to the strength and wellbeing of the team. It quickly became the hub of prayer and fellowship, as well as strategic development and day-to-day planning. Staff members travelled great distances across the city to attend meetings, often in intense heat and discomfort, but their efforts were well worth it in terms of the fellowship and spiritual strength that was apparent in those early years. The personal friendships and loyalty between local and expatriate staff was a witness to Christian unity and the commitment they had to one another. The annual conferences, when all the staff from Bombay and Bangalore came together for teaching, prayer and fellowship were always a high point each year.

Most staff members and volunteers were young and unmarried, and it came as no surprise when a number of Anglo Indian marriages became a possibility and then a reality. However, members of Frontline Teams were not allowed to develop serious relationships with other team members (or local Christians) of the opposite sex, until their period as team members had ended. Needless to say, a number of future marriages grew out of this, notwithstanding the attitude of some traditional missionary societies, some of whom had advised Oasis, in the light of their own experience, against allowing cross-cultural relationships to develop. It seemed to the Oasis Leadership, however, that it made little sense to preach that all were equal and "one in Christ Jesus" and at the same time discourage marriage, the highest and most explicit form of unity and acceptance. However, in the light of the advice they had received, the Leadership were at pains to address some of the practical issues that needed to be faced, and to introduce appropriate procedures to overcome cultural differences which might otherwise stand in the way of successful marriages.

The early years in India were marked by a strong vision of what God was calling Oasis to do, the commitment of one staff member to another, strong cross-cultural links, dedication to the needs of the poor, all of which were under-girded by prayer. Such prayer was essential for all the usual reasons, but also because obstacles to the development of the work became increasingly severe over time, as the political environment became less benign and at times even hostile.

Three examples of answered prayer out of many, offer just a taste of how God worked in those early days. In order to get projects off the ground, it was essential that most of the seed money should come from the UK and other western countries. A large number of people visited India as team members, and the interest of 'partner' churches, coupled with exciting new projects such as Purnata Bhavan, attracted a high level of giving, including grants from large Trusts and Foundations. Significant sums of money became available both for the infrastructure and for project running costs. However, government permission was needed to bring foreign funds into India and this was not readily forthcoming. After much hard work and in a dramatic answer to prayer, permission was received just one week before the project was due to launch.

Second, Oasis India quickly came up against the problems of corruption and, in particular, bribery and the black economy. As a result of this, it proved extremely difficult to lease premises for the Jacob's Well manufacturing and training project to which Oasis had been committed and for which Ruth Cox had returned to India. Many months went by as suitable premises were sought, only to be rejected because of the unwillingness of Oasis to compromise its high standards of integrity. However, by March 1994 suitable premises were found in Bandra, central Bombay, owned by an Indian Muslim, who readily leased the premises at an acceptable rent and without underhand dealings.

Thirdly, the story of Purnata Bhavan in Igatpuri, some 120kms outside Bombay, is a monument to the faithfulness of God in answering prayer and bringing about changes beyond normal human expectations or probability. In 1994 Andy met with John Nonhebel and Graham Mungeam in a café in Bombay. They were discussing the next steps in the work of Oasis in India, and Andy felt strongly that something should be done to help women and their children who had been rejected by society because they had become infected by the HIV virus. Such women were known to church leaders, and it was decided to set up a home outside the city which would restore their self-worth, attempt to withstand the onset of full blown AIDS, and provide education and training for their children. It was an ambitious project requiring some £175,000 to be raised. The full story of Purnata Bhavan may be told elsewhere. Suffice to say that the leadership in Bombay felt that some seven 'miracles'- defined as difficult, even impossible events requiring God to work in very special ways - were required if the project were to come to fruition. In the event, a new Indian Christian, Philip Lobo, who had recently come to faith whilst serving a prison sentence for offences he had not committed, and who was now attending the 'Valley of Praise' church in Bombay, was used by God to make what seemed a virtual impossibility a reality. Philip had been introduced to Andy by Ivan Raskino, the pastor of that church, who had hosted the first Frontline team in Bombay. Ivan had also helped Ruth birth the vision for 'Jacobs Well' and played a key role in encouraging Oasis in those early years.

After inspecting and praying over a possible site in Igatpuri on 1 January 1995, the first phase of Purnata Bhavan was opened in March 1997 and the remaining phases by 2000. The seven "miracles" had occurred - a testimony to the faithfulness of God

There were many moments of doubt and uncertainty as Purnata Bhavan got off the ground, but the commandment to "*look after orphans and widows in their distress*" (James 1:27) was always a compelling influence.

Europe

While Oasis India was being established, Frontline Teams were being sent to an increasing number of countries. The UK leadership team had in 1990, identified ten major cities, including Paris and Berlin, which it was felt might in due course provide suitable locations for Oasis work. Europe was in a state of transition. The Soviet Union had broken up, the Berlin Wall had come down, the European Community was expanding, and transport links with the Continent were about to be transformed by the Channel Tunnel. It seemed natural, therefore, that Oasis in the UK should begin to think about the needs of its nearest neighbours, and France was the first country to present itself. Although only twenty miles away from the White Cliffs of Dover, in recent years it had been largely neglected as a mission field.

Dominique Sublet was a student from France studying at Leeds University. She became a Christian at one of the many missions conducted by Steve. Lacking any enthusiasm to return to France at the end of her studies, she joined the first Frontline team in India and on her return to the UK applied to Oasis to become a housing support worker at No. 3. Whilst at the hostel, and despite her reluctance to return to France, Dominique sensed that God was calling her back to her home country. She had felt great antipathy to the Catholic Church in France but now her attitudes were being changed and she began to feel that, perhaps, it would be through the church in France that her country would emerge from its humanistic and secular past. As a result, when the Oasis Leadership let it be known that Oasis was considering sending teams to Paris, Dominique was the first to come forward. A base was established at a church in Belleville, close to the Gard du Nord, which at the time was led by the Rev. Charlie Cleverly, a Crosslinks missionary from the UK. Belleville was a socially deprived area with a large immigrant community. It had a history of UK missionary involvement, but had proved to be a difficult area for Christian ministry. Teams were also sent to other churches and organisations in the city and efforts were made to introduce forms of social outreach of the kind now operating in the UK and India.

The going proved extremely difficult however and, after some years, little progress had been made in establishing a permanent base, though teams had helped local churches, including the one at Belleville. The decision was taken to suspend the work at least for the time being. Dominique subsequently married a French pastor, and Charlie Cleverly returned to a church in the UK. Although at the time the closure of the work was disappointing, good work had been done and lessons had been learnt which would stand Oasis in good stead in the years to come.

In Germany, a number of links were established with some churches in East Berlin through an English lawyer who had been present when the Berlin wall came down. He approached Oasis to see if work could be started amongst the young people of Berlin. He had been greatly moved by their need as he saw their godlessness and hopelessness after so many years of atheistic communism. Various initiatives were taken but little substantive progress was made.

FTA Teams also went to Lisbon, Portugal, for several years, and later to Romania and Belgium. But it was clear that none of these provided, at the time, sufficiently strong environments for the establishment of permanent Oasis work in Europe. One possible explanation was the Overseas Department's preoccupation with the developing work in India and Brazil. This left few resources for these early European initiatives. A more concentrated and dedicated approach was needed. Thus, in 2003 Phil Lane, who had previously worked in India, was appointed as European Development Director for Oasis, based in Belgium. The time seemed right to move into Europe again.

Brazil

Despite the disappointments in Europe, much was taking place elsewhere. Christmas Cracker grants had been made to support street children in Brazil, and Oasis had links to São Paulo through the Rev Stuart Christine, who was committed to church planting in the Favelas (slums) of the city. Stuart had been Director of the Oasis/Spurgeons course in Church Planting and Evangelism that commenced in 1990 (see Chapter 6). On his return to Brazil, he became the driving force behind the 'Associação Batista de Incentivo e Apoio ao Homem' or ABIAH, translated as the 'Baptist Association for Community Support and Encouragement'.

The organisation had been set up as a result of the vision of a Brazilian couple, Antonio and Sonia Costa, who had seen the enormous needs in the favelas of the city. Although there were many organisations helping the numerous children living on the streets of São Paulo, it was felt that a more effective long-term approach would be to give education to pre-school children before they found themselves at the mercy of street life with all its desolation and violence.

Whilst teaching at the Baptist Theological Seminary, Stuart together with his wife, Georgie, who was a teacher, set up a pilot pre-school in one of the favela communities. It proved to be highly successful so was immediately replicated in other locations in the city as an instrument for planting new churches. The vision of ABIAH was essentially akin to the vision of Oasis, and teams from England began to visit the city, both from Oasis and from the Baptist Missionary Society. (Earlier Oasis had assisted the BMS in setting up its own overseas teams programme under the name 'Action Teams') The Oasis and BMS teams worked together, mapping out potential areas, visiting slum homes to determine need, and helping to start new pre-schools. They also made a significant contribution in helping to build the ABIAH central base and offices in Jardim Olinda on the edge of a slum. Some team members went to São Jose dos Campos, a town close to São Paulo, where they supported a large Baptist Church in an innovative form of evangelism- a travelling 'circus' tent which moved from place to place offering a range of services, such as dentistry, entertainment, and opportunities for local residents to hear about the Christian faith.

In 1996, Graham Mungeam visited Brazil and met with the ABIAH trustees. He discussed the possibility of a closer association between Oasis in the UK and ABIAH, as well as other contacts in Brazil who had been the recipients of Cracker grants. Steve also visited the country to produce a Cracker video. This showed the stark contrasts between the lives of the rich and the poor in that vast country, and was used to encourage participation in the following year's project. Subsequently, Pastor Francisco Nilo, the Executive Secretary of ABIAH, visited Oasis in London. The two organisations agreed to work in partnership and to adopt the name ABIAH Oasis.

At this time thought was also being given to the possibility of starting work in Peru, a Spanish speaking country, which might in due course open up opportunities in the rest of Spanish speaking South America. With the help of Latin Link, FTA teams visited a number of locations. An Oasis couple also visited the country to explore the possibilities for starting a new base. Sadly, they had to return to the UK prematurely because of ill health and the matter was not pursued.

Elsewhere, Oasis had established contacts in Mozambique and Frontline teams were visiting Beira on a regular basis when visiting Zimbabwe. The legacy of Portuguese colonisation meant that Portuguese was spoken in a number of countries in Africa, including Mozambique. In the light of the Brazilian church's commitment to worldwide mission, it became clear to both ABIAH and Oasis that their new association had the potential to produce a powerful combination in Portuguese speaking countries, and particularly, in this context, Mozambique. In 2001, ABIAH established pre-school work in Mozambique, supported by Oasis staff from the UK. Meanwhile, ABIAH Oasis had become a full member of the Oasis family in 1998.

Zimbabwe and Mozambique

The story of Oasis in Zimbabwe is a particular testimony to the way in which God uses events, sometimes tragic, to bring about His purposes. In the early days of Christmas Cracker, a grant was made to a young woman, Gail Decker, the leader of a YWAM project for street children in Beira, Mozambique. Gail's parents, Rikki and Margaret Decker, had pioneered the Greystone Park Christian Fellowship in Harare, Zimbabwe, and the church had played a key role in acquiring and renovating a building as a base for work among the children in Beira. Gail and a friend had cared for some fifty street boys from their flat until the building came on stream. It was given the name Casa Re-om - the House of the Lord my Shepherd.

In 1994 news reached the UK that Gail had been tragically killed by a buffalo on her honeymoon, following her marriage to John Wickes, an American missionary working in Beira. Margaret Decker tells the story of Gail's life in the book "A Grain of Wheat"[1]. Christmas Cracker sent a gift to the fund set up in Gail's memory and the money was used to support Casa Re-om and Kedesh, a home for post primary children providing vocational training that John had set up.

Back in the UK, the Oasis Leadership had a meeting with John Barron who had resigned from local government service to set up the Share Trust to support his ministry to poor pastors in Zimbabwe. John regularly spent six months in Zimbabwe and six months in the UK. He had heard about Christmas Cracker and was attracted by its emphasis on the support of causes which were too small to attract donations from the large Christian aid and development organisations. At the end of the meeting, John Barron agreed that he would encourage the mainly white churches in Harare, which he knew well, to set up Cracker projects of their own. His aims were to bring black and white churches, and particularly their young people, together around a common project, to provide an insight into the needs of the poor on their doorstep, and to encourage them to do something effective about them. Six churches subsequently took part with exciting results. One of the leading figures was a youth leader in the Highlands Presbyterian Church named Andy Shaw, who saw the potential of Christmas

[1] Published by New Wine Press

108

Cracker and over two years raised awareness through TV and radio. He also inspired the churches to work together for the benefit of the poor and marginalised. Andy was subsequently murdered while praying alone one morning, and much of the impetus of the project was lost. He had played a key part in the success of the project and in the future development of work in Zimbabwe. One church set up work in the slums of Harare; and another sought to help the Batonka tribe who had been displaced by the massive Kariba Dam project in the course of construction.

The ground had been laid for the first UK Frontline Team to visit Harare. Judy Coles, the FTA project manager, with the help of John Barron, established links with Rikki Decker at the Greystone Park Christian Fellowship, and teams began to go to Harare on a regular basis.

Each year the teams visited John Wickes, Gail's husband, in Mozambique, during their stay in Harare. John was a man of great faith, character and courage. He had continued to run the project after Gail's untimely death. Each year he made a profound impression on FTA team members. He galvanised many of them to new commitment and new service, setting an example that left a deep impression on his young visitors. The Oasis link with Kedesh was to become stronger in due course as volunteers were seconded and as permanent Oasis staff arrived in the country.

By 1998, it seemed appropriate to explore whether a more permanent base for Oasis could be established in Harare. Accompanied by John Barron, Graham Mungeam visited Harare to see whether the right conditions existed, staying with Rikki and Margaret Decker and being introduced to key people in the city. The country was, even then, showing signs of political instability, economic decline and social disorder.

It was clear that there were many needs and opportunities, not least the huge numbers of young people leaving school without work and the equally alarming number of young people orphaned by HIV/AIDS. Graham was surprised, however, at what appeared to him to be a lack of racial integration, even within the churches. During his stay serious riots occurred in downtown Harare, and it seemed clear that things were likely to get worse before they got better. However, he was greatly encouraged by a prayer meeting of some 400 black pastors and a few white pastors, in the centre of Harare, to which Rikki Decker invited him. Food shortages were becoming endemic and the pastors called on God's help for the nation at what was a critical time in its life. Rikki had the faith and vision to see that the troubled times in which the nation found itself provided a wonderful opportunity for God to work in new ways.

On his return to the UK, Graham reported that Oasis should seek to establish a base but only with the support of local churches and subject to the active involvement of all sections of the community. He believed that further work should be undertaken to the end.

With the arrival of Tim Jeffery in 1999 to head up the Oasis Overseas Department (soon to be renamed Global Action), the scene was set for significant new developments. Tim had himself had family connections with Zimbabwe and he immediately sought to establish a long-term base. With the support of funds from Philadelphia in the States, and the recruitment back into Oasis of Stephen and Joanna Jack from the UK, an Oasis Zimbabwe base would finally become a reality. Stephen had previously been involved with Frontline teams in the UK and after a period of nursing was well equipped to set up something new and challenging. Stephen launched a youth training programme, ran the Frontline teams and began to develop some key formative church partnerships. For children at risk, a number of pre-schools were begun, and detached work amongst street girls in the centre of Harare became an established part of the fledgling organisation's activities. Stephen also drove forward a residential and vocational training project based in a redundant hotel that became known as 'OSTA', the Oasis Skills Training Academy.

The organisation was sufficiently well established early in the new decade to set up a shadow board and later became an officially registered organisation. In 2005 it became the fifth Oasis country to join the International Council.

Discussions also took place early in the decade between the UK and Stuart Christine in Brazil about the possibility of joint work in Mozambique. The pre-school education programme, PEPE, run in São Paulo and other parts of Brazil, was being set up in conjunction with the Mozambique Baptist Association, whilst a number of young people from the UK had gone to work with John Wickes in Kedesh. The time seemed to be right for a joint Brazil/UK initiative.

In 2000 Jim and Jane Currell completed an assignment with Oasis India in Bangalore where Jane had taught in the schools and Jim had set up a vocational training project. Following two years at All Nations Christian College, they were keen to stay with Oasis but to pioneer work in a new location. Tim Jeffery encouraged them to consider Mozambique and after a visit with members of their supporting church, they felt this was a place where they could make a difference. Following a time of language study in Portugal they left for Beira in 2002 and began to develop new ministry focused around empowering local churches.

It had been part of Oasis policy to give young people experience of mission before, rather than after, full time training. This was partly a matter of practicalities - young people were often called to mission as a result of their gap-year experiences - but also out of the belief that training could be of greater value when given in the context of hard experience gained on the field. Thus, over the years, a number of couples - John and Charmaine Nonhebel in India, Dave and Preeti How in Bangladesh and Jim and Jane Currell, all attended two years of training at All Nations Christian College. In addition a number of Oasis India staff, Tim Shinde from Bombay, and Clifford Ghanakan and Rajshekher from Bangalore, came to England to study on the Oasis Youth Ministry Course in preparation for ministry in India.

Bases were now in place in both Zimbabwe and Mozambique and developments had also been taking place in Uganda.

Uganda

The work in Uganda was started by Ceri Duncan, who had been a member of a Frontline Team to Bangalore in 1996/97. Following her time in India, Ceri joined the Oasis London office as the FTA Project Manager responsible for investigating new countries for team placements. With the help of the Chairman of the charity 'Send a Cow', whose daughter had been a member of an Oasis team to Europe, Ceri visited Uganda to assess the possibilities for teams in East Africa. The results were UK teams to Mozambique and Kenya in October 1999.

As Ceri became increasingly involved, she felt God was calling her to that part of the world, and she was therefore pleased to be sent to Kampala in 2001 to oversee team placements in East Africa. There she saw numerous girls at risk in the city and began to research their needs. After six months, a small house was rented in a slum area of the city and a structured day care programme for street girls was introduced.

The work grew rapidly and it was not long before the Bambejja (translated 'Princesses') project was touching the lives of many girls at risk, some of whom had lived on the streets and others who were in danger of doing so. Ceri initially carried the burden on her own and although short-term teams and other volunteers came to help, there was clearly a need for sustainable long-term arrangements.

It was for this reason that Ruth and Matthew Visick-Evans took on the role of base Directors in 2003, freeing up Ceri to concentrate on the project she had set up. Ruth had joined Oasis in the UK from Cambridge City Council, and had worked in the Oasis Community Action Department as its Research and Development Manager. Matthew had held several senior financial posts in the Phillips Electronics Group. Other new members of staff followed and by 2004 the foundations had been laid for the development of several initiatives in addition to Bambejja. Ruth & Matthew concentrated their efforts on building organisational capacity which was essential for Oasis Uganda if it was, in due course, to become a full member of the International Council. Before that could happen, however, it was essential that Ugandans themselves took on management and leadership positions. This proved difficult, and raised questions which needed to be addressed, not just in Uganda but in other countries as well.

By 2004, Oasis work in Uganda was touching the lives of over one hundred girls through the Bambejja Project. This now consisted of four elements - a child support programme offering day school and welfare services; a pre-settlement programme for nine girls who were HIV orphans; a vocational skills training centre for 24 young men and teenage girls; and a family empowerment programme linked with local churches. There was also a successful Net2Work programme and visits by Global Action teams. In all there were about fifty full-time, part-time and volunteer staff working with Oasis in Uganda at the end of 2004.

Oasis, though still small, now had seminal work in three countries of Africa.

USA

Andy Matheson left India in the spring of 2000 after 21 years associated with the Interserve organisation, first as a teacher at Woodstock School and then for eight year as the first Director of Oasis India. By that time he had been appointed to succeed Graham Mungeam, on his retirement as International Director of Oasis in July 2001. It was agreed that, before taking up the post, he would spend a year in the United States studying at the Fuller Theological Seminary in Pasadena.

During his initial months at Fuller, Andy realised the potential for building up a US base to support inner city work in Los Angeles and other parts of the world. Having obtained the agreement of Oasis UK, Oasis India and Oasis Brazil, he set about exploring how to set up the necessary legal framework and make appropriate contacts. At the same time, Andy took a course in Board Management in order to explore and understand the most effective models for board governance. During the course of that study, his tutor, Shelley Trebesch, voiced her commitment to the vision of Oasis and a willingness to be involved in setting up a US operation. Andy proceeded to get in touch with two other people whom he knew were supportive of the idea - Bill Young, who had visited the work in India on several occasions when his daughter, Lindsey Potter, had been involved; and John Rusk, a local pastor whom he had got to know during classes which they had shared together at Fuller. The three agreed to be the founding directors of Oasis USA, incorporated in the State of California. Having registered, they began to plan strategically, to acquire charitable status and to appoint staff. After a search process, Scott Engmann was appointed in July 2002 as Oasis USA's first Chief Executive. Scott began to acquaint himself with the work of Oasis in different parts of the world, and to network interested people and organisations. Before long the first Oasis USA teams were being sent to other parts of the world. Work was also planned for inner city Los Angeles and for a Net2work computer project amongst the poor in New Mexico.

Oasis USA, with the nation's resources and history of mission activity, clearly had the potential to become a major player in the Oasis global family to which it was formally admitted in 2002.

Bangladesh

In 1998 Dave and Preeti How, who had been working with Oasis India in Bombay for some time, began to look at possible options for the establishment of a new Oasis base in India. Having visited Kanpur in the north and Calcutta in the east, Andy put a proposal to the India Board suggesting that Dave and Preeti might head up a new team in one of these locations. To prepare themselves for this, Dave and Preeti returned to the UK and underwent a period of training at All Nations Christian College. In the event the India Board decided not to proceed with a new base and Andy suggested that Oasis might look alternatively at Dhaka in Bangladesh. This was in line with Graham Mungeam's sense of God's leading. As the newly appointed International Director, Graham had been invited to Interserve's Annual UK Conference at Swanwick in part because of the growing links between the two organisations. Having attended a seminar on the Lamb Hospital in Bangladesh, he was impressed by the fact that the country, though largely Muslim, was still officially a secular state and ready to receive appropriately skilled workers from abroad. Bangladesh was also one of the poorest countries in the world and, being surrounded on three sides by India, would be easily accessible to Oasis staff from Bombay or Bangalore. He wondered, therefore, if this country with its then 123 million inhabitants might be the next area in which Oasis might establish a presence. He was encouraged to think further along these lines when, whilst in India, he unexpectedly met the President of the Bangladesh Bible Society who encouraged him to pursue the idea.

Andy visited Dhaka in February 2000 and was followed on an exploratory visit by Dave and Preeti later that year. During this visit they began to see the enormous needs and opportunities in that city of over ten million people. The International Council was asked to approve the idea and Dave and Preeti began planning their move to Dhaka. They did not know at that stage where or with whom they would be working. In the following year, the Chairman and Chief Executive of Koinonia (an organisation not dissimilar to Oasis) invited Graham Mungeam to pay a fact finding visit to Dhaka and to see the situation in the country for himself. During that visit, he met a number of people who, with the passage of time, proved to be supportive of the establishment of an Oasis presence in the country. One important contact was David Halder, the Executive Director of HELP Bangladesh, an NGO based on the outskirts of Dhaka City. Oasis was subsequently invited to establish a partnership with HELP and to set up a vocational training and small business enterprise unit on HELP's campus.

The other two members of the new team in Dhaka were Stephan and Elisabeth Blanc. Jeannie Herbert, who was an Interserve partner seconded to Oasis in Bombay, had met Stephan and Elisabeth at the home of mutual friends in Switzerland. On hearing that they were interested in Bangladesh and were going to study at Fuller, Jeannie suggested that they should make contact with Andy. As a textile engineer, Stephan seemed ideally suited to the requirements of a country 76% of whose exports were produced by the garment industry. He and Elisabeth became partners with Interserve on their return to Switzerland and were duly seconded to work with Oasis in Dhaka

Global Action Teams

The main driving forces behind the development of Oasis activities abroad in the 1990s were the Christmas Cracker project and the UK's Frontline Teams Abroad programme, later renamed 'Global Action Teams'. The latter developed as a key vehicle for opening up and consolidating new opportunities. In 2004 some 200 young people, anxious to serve God abroad, were due to take part in the many options to the many countries then on offer.

Another key development was the Net2Work Project financed initially by the Department for International Development (DfID). This was introduced by the UK into a number of countries, starting in Brazil and India, offering computer training to poor young people in the cities in which Oasis had bases, and beyond. Together they provided a vital stimulus to the consolidation and expansion of the Oasis family throughout the world.

It became clear very early on, however, that it would be neither appropriate nor practicable for the UK to own and control Oasis work across the world. New structures for bringing about a global family of Oasis centres were needed. These are discussed in the following chapter.

Chapter 9
A Global Family

The decision taken in 1994 to allow the work in India to operate as a legal entity, entirely independent of the UK, was of far reaching importance. It was recognised that historical models of mission activity, based on command and control from the UK, were no longer appropriate in the post-colonial era. Other models needed to be developed which offered full independence on the one hand, but a firm commitment to Oasis beliefs, values and practices on the other.

A Global Strategy

The issues, and the challenges that they posed to successful and harmonious work in the future, were considered at a meeting between the leaders of Oasis UK and Oasis India in the autumn of 1996 when a strategy was formulated designed to reconcile the conflicting factors. The agreed strategy was to set up independent Oasis organisations, similar to Oasis India, in Africa, South America and Continental Europe, each with the potential to develop ministries to other countries in their respective areas of operation.

The separate bodies would be of equal standing and status and would be brought together by an International Council on which all the countries concerned would be represented. A small "secretariat" headed up by an International Director would serve this. The Council would deal with policy matters, particularly strategic development, and those matters best addressed at an international level. The aim was to have a global family working together, praying together, learning together and supporting one another.

The Case for Independence

The case for setting up independent national Oasis organisations was based on the leadership's understanding of biblical teaching and practical considerations. There were five principal arguments.

Biblically it was argued that each Oasis organisation should stand in a servant relationship with all the others, recognising that no individual national ministry was more important than any other. Following the Pauline teaching on the Church, whilst each national organisation may have ministries which were in some senses different from those of others, they were all 'one body', dependent on one another and sharing one another's joys and sorrows.

This principle of equality posed particularly challenging questions in its application for historical reasons and because of the disparity between the resources of the developing nations and those of the Western World. However, legal structures were set in place designed to reflect the ideal that Oasis was seeking to achieve.

The second consideration was the need to ensure that the holistic gospel was demonstrated in *culturally appropriate* and sensitive ways. It was agreed that the national church was best placed to understand and meet the needs of the country concerned, an argument forcibly made in respect of Asia in " Revolution in World Mission: The Changing Face of Mission" by Dr YP Yohannan[1], Founder of Gospel for Asia. Another book "Mosques and Miracles" by Dr Stuart Robinson[2] also makes the case strongly in relation to the Islamic world. This meant significant changes in the role of western agencies, not least in developing national leaders, and passing responsibility on to them. The leadership of Oasis was convinced that this was the best way to rapidly increase its impact in different parts of the world.

Thirdly, there were *political considerations*. Many countries had been closed to Western missionaries for some time and in others visas were becoming increasingly difficult to obtain. International conflict

[1] Published by Gates of Praise

[2] Published by CityHarvest Publications

and political and social instability also posed a threat in many countries. Oasis organisations, led and run by nationals, could overcome many if not all of these difficulties.

Another consideration was the need for Oasis organisations to become financially independent, at least after an initial period when seed corn and start- up help would be needed. This might seem to fly in the face of the principle of inter-dependence or, indeed, the clear willingness of Oasis supporters in Western countries to give generously to those in need in the developing world. On the other hand, it was important not to encourage a dependency culture. The adage "He who pays the piper calls the tune" could be as true in the Christian world as it clearly was in the secular. It seemed right to the Oasis Leadership that those who rightly and properly received help from others should ultimately enjoy the self-respect and confidence which financial independence brings.

Finally, it was clear, even in those early days that as the Oasis work expanded into different parts of the world it would be impossible for control to be exercised from London or any other part of the UK. In *practical terms* independent developments were inevitable and it would be better for such developments to take place within a framework agreed by the parties concerned and not in an ad hoc manner.

The International Council

The first meeting of the Council was held in Bangalore, India in September 1998. There were just three countries involved, Oasis India, Oasis ABIAH and Oasis UK. There were those who suggested that it was premature to set up an international organisation whilst the number of Oasis bodies was so small. On the other hand, Oasis leaders felt that it would be far easier for three countries to agree on the basic principles underlying Oasis globally and the rules for international cooperation, than to wait for the participation of others, however welcome on other grounds that might be.

The meeting lasted for two days and was chaired by Pastor James Salins, the Chairman of Oasis India and the pastor of a church with ministry in Ganashpada, a slum in the Marol area of Bombay. The meeting opened with prayer and devotions and time was allocated to each delegation to explain their national ministries. Although some

118

members of the Council knew one another, for others time was needed to break down natural reserve and to develop mutual confidence.
Some 13 papers were discussed including those which were historical
and descriptive, those which set out a draft two year strategy for development, and those designed to obtain the Council's agreement on practical matters, including a budget and the appointment of the
International Director. However, by far the most important paper was
that which set out for discussion the underlying principles and values
of the Oasis family and the way the members would relate to one
another.

Underlying Principles

It was clear that if the concept of the Oasis family was to have any
meaning it could only do so if each country held certain common
underlying beliefs and principles. The unity had to go beyond the use
of the name Oasis. These unifying factors needed to be agreed not only
to give unity and cohesion to the members of the organisation, but also
to provide criteria that others would need to meet if applying to join
the Council in due course. At the most fundamental level it was their
shared belief in the tenets of the Christian faith and the unity that they
shared in Christ, which bound the organisations together. It was agreed
that rather than attempt to write a new Oasis statement of faith, the
organisation would adopt the 'Statement of Faith' of the Evangelical
Missionary Alliance (later to become 'Global Connections'). The
Council also agreed to subscribe to the Lausanne Covenant that had
been drawn up in the seventies by Christian leaders of many nations.

The Council also attempted to define more clearly what distin-
guished Oasis ministries from those of other similar organisations.
These characteristics had been discussed in the UK early in 1995 on
the basis of a paper written by Andy Matheson. It was agreed that
Oasis was committed to holistic mission and would concentrate its
work mainly in urban areas. It would work in and through local
churches at their invitation and not, under any circumstances, be in
competition with them. The principal emphasis would be on the needs
of poor and marginalised children and young people: those who were
the poorest of the poor and often regarded by some as the dregs of society.

The Council also agreed that collectively it would be committed to cross-cultural ministry - 'from everywhere to everywhere' and no longer be limited to 'the West to the rest' - as had been typical of much mission activity over the previous two hundred years.

Having agreed these principles the Council was still faced with the question of how it could ensure in the years that lay ahead that member organisations lived by them and, even more challenging, that new members bearing the name 'Oasis' did not operate in ways which were at variance with such fundamental tenets. In other words, how could the integrity of the organisation be maintained? In response to this, a number of conditions were set for membership of the Council and sanctions agreed for any Oasis country that might fail to live up to what had been agreed.

The 1998 Council decided that these and the many other issues that had been discussed in outline needed further thinking and refinement. The newly appointed International Director was therefore asked to work on these proposals and to bring them to the next Council meeting scheduled for São Paulo, Brazil in 2000. Both the 2000 meeting and the meeting held in London in 2002 devoted much time to considering these issues and the wider strategic development of Oasis work across the world. In preparation, Bob Morris, the ex Chairman of the Interserve International Council in Toronto, Canada, was consulted about the way that particular organisation had become an effective family over the years. Central to this was the drawing up of a draft Covenant which Graham Mungeam presented to the Council in Brazil. This effectively brought together all that had been agreed, and represented a form of 'Constitution' to which all new members of the Oasis family would be asked to subscribe (the Covenant is reproduced in Appendix C).

The São Paulo conference of 2000 agreed that Andy Matheson, currently at Fuller Theological Seminary, should succeed Graham Mungeam as International Director on the latter's retirement in 2001. It also decided that it would be helpful for a number of reasons if the Council operated within a formal legal framework. This process proved more difficult than had been expected but the Oasis International Association was registered as a company in 2001 and obtained charitable status in 2003. Graham Mungeam was invited to be Chairman of the Council and of the Company. His close association with Andy Matheson over many years and his previous involvement in the development of Oasis work overseas provided a basis for growth and continuity.

From the first meeting of the Council in Bangalore in 1998 it had been the intention to ensure that the Council was truly international and not dominated by the British. The early appointments belied this, but the intention remained ultimately to replace the Council's first officers with leaders from countries across the world. UK law required, however, that the Oasis International Association had a majority of British directors so at an early meeting it was resolved that all future decisions (subject only to legal requirements) would be devolved to the International Council in which the UK was a minority voice.

By the time of the fourth meeting of the Council, this time in Goa, India in 2004, the USA had been added to the three founder members of Brazil, India and the UK. Representatives from Bangladesh were present as observers, as were colleagues from Zimbabwe, Mozambique and Uganda, where work was being carried out under the auspices of the UK. Once they obtained legal status in their own countries, independent of the UK, they too would become full members of the Council. The Council decided at the meeting that it would aim to develop Oasis work across the world so that, by the year 2010, God willing, the Oasis Global family would consist of twelve independent countries.

Chapter 10
What to say and how to say it

From its inception, Steve knew what he wanted Oasis to proclaim to the world at large, but he still needed to explore how this could best be achieved. He recognised that traditional methods of communication such as teaching and preaching in church, speaking in the open air, one to one conversations etc., had their proper place; but when it came to reaching the mass of the population, other methods had to be found. This applied particularly to the increasing number of young people who rarely if ever attended the nation's churches. He realised that however powerful and effective the message, there was little point in proclaiming it if no one was listening, and he became convinced that "actions speak louder than words". If Christians were to be salt and light, they had to be fully involved in the life of society.

From his early days as a student at Spurgeons College and later in his ministries at Gravesend and Tonbridge, Steve explored how best to present the message in innovative, attractive and challenging ways. He was always toying with new ideas and new approaches. Initially he frequented pubs (something which may not seem remarkable today, but which was largely frowned upon by many evangelical churches in the early '80s) working with a Christian band. Later, whilst at Tonbridge, he began to use multi media presentations, of the kind especially enjoyed by young people, to get the message across. Drama and comedy were also seen as having an important role to play.

One of the features of the early nationwide evangelistic projects, 'Christmas Unwrapped' and 'On Fire', was a deliberate and sustained effort to promote through the media what the projects were all about, and to raise the profile of the church in the public's mind. Similarly, the 'Christmas Cracker' projects of 1991and 1992 used the medium of local radio to raise funds and draw attention to the problems of the developing world.

Good communications and marketing were also needed at another level. If Oasis was to be effective in communicating the Christian faith throughout the UK, it needed to learn how to project and market itself, in order to make the young organisation better known in the Christian world and beyond, and to attract gifted and committed Christians to its ranks. A precondition for this was high quality publicity and promotion - something that the Christian world did not at that time always understand or appreciate.

Accordingly, Oasis began to look for someone who could help it to meet this need. In the event, the post was filled by Nick Page, a gifted writer, who had authored many of the scripts used by the Ambush Theatre Company. On its break-up in 1999, Nick had joined the Baptist Times as a reporter, working out of the Baptist Union complex in Didcot. There he had met Steve, who visited on a regular basis, and who invited him to join Oasis to take charge of publicity and marketing. His task was to develop a communications strategy, write copy, develop publicity, prepare press releases, and write material for Shout Theatre Company.

On his arrival in January 1990, Nick invited each project leader to set out in twenty words what each project was about. This gave him a clear understanding of Oasis and he was immediately struck by the range and diversity of its work. Having obtained this information he immediately took steps to produce new publicity and a new newsletter. He also began to develop the art of drafting promotional and fundraising letters for Steve, thus releasing Steve for his other duties.

Over time Nick wrote a number of books in partnership with Steve. These included 'Sex Matters', a young person's guide, which served as a useful complementary resource to Steve's video, produced for Scripture Union, called 'Lessons in Love'. Nick also wrote for other organisations, in order to bring in money to strengthen the Trust's finances.

As head of the Media Department, Nick did much to bring a young, vibrant and humorous (even at times, quirky) feel to Oasis publicity and promotion. In September 1991 a management review suggested that to increase further the effectiveness of the Trust's marketing and publicity, he should join the Leadership team. This strengthened the team by bringing together policy and marketing, but also introduced his unique brand of humour into the team's proceedings, which was to prove a particular blessing at times of stress and uncertainty.

Up until 1990 Oasis commissioned much of its design work from outside specialists. This was expensive and often less than satisfactory on a number of grounds. Someone in-house was needed who would devote themselves exclusively to design. The solution came quickly and from an unexpected source. Amongst the 'prizes' offered by the 1989 Christmas Cracker project was the opportunity for the winning team to have a meal with Steve in London's Covent Garden. One such prizewinner was Erol Rezvan, a young graphic designer from Ipswich who had been out of work for some months. Although Erol had a good portfolio, potential employers had repeatedly rejected him. Following its policy of, wherever possible, giving people a chance to develop their gifting, Erol was offered a job in Oasis. It soon became clear that he would be able to provide precisely the imaginative and colourful designs that Oasis needed. Erol was to become a key player in Oasis for several years, producing work that was admired both inside and outside the confines of the organisation.

In its search for modernity and relevance, Oasis had to struggle with a number of issues as it sought to express the unchanging message of the Gospel in a way that would be well received in the rapidly changing world of modern youth. For instance, the term 'evangelism' was not one with which many young Christians were familiar, and carried certain unhelpful connotations. The leadership decided that, in its dealings with the outside world, it would speak instead of 'communicating' the Christian message, and the department concerned was named the Communication Department. This however led to all manner of difficulties as churches and others thought they were dealing with the department responsible for marketing and publicity rather than that concerned with evangelism. The name was eventually dropped in favour of 'mission' despite the latter's ambiguity. However, the concept of communicating the Christian message in various ways took hold, and the word 'evangelism' was rarely used. This had significant advantages when discussions were taking place with statutory authorities and others who were suspicious of Oasis' proselytising activities, as they saw them.

Oasis also continued to seek out the most effective way of communicating with people using the new information technologies. It was the first, or one of the first, Christian organisations to set up a website and this paved the way for the even more ambitious use of the technologies through Church.co.uk and Xalt (see Chapter 3).

Steve's early books were closely associated with his role as a youth speaker and leader. His first, "The Complete Youth Manual", was written in 1987 and was followed in 1991 and 1992 by "Understanding Teenagers" and "The Christian Youth Manual". Similarly, the "Christmas Cracker" manual was written in 1990 as a key tool in the newly launched Christmas Cracker project. During this time he was also committed to monthly articles on Youth Leadership and other Christian journals. These articles often formed the material for subsequent books.

Many of Steve's later books were written in co-operation with others with expertise in the subject concerned. In particular, early in the 1990s, Oasis employed Paul Hansford as co-author and researcher. Paul had graduated from London Bible College (now the London School of Theology) and did much of the theological and other groundwork, providing a crucial extra resource to enable Steve to devote himself to writing and his other activities.

Many of the new books continued to be linked with Oasis projects and Steve's preoccupations at the time. For instance, a new and separate charity, 'Parentalk', was set up out of Oasis in 1999, and Steve edited, and wrote with others, more than fifteen books on issues across a wide range of parenting topics. The 'Faithworks' initiative also required resources and Steve devoted himself to a range of material designed to underpin its work and explain its rationale.

Some books, however, were written with a wider audience in mind. In 1995 Steve sought to explain the Christian faith to a readership of those who were seeking the truth but struggling to find it. "More than Meets the Eye" was an early attempt to explain profound ideas in a way that unchurched readers could understand. Together with a Scripture Union video "Good Question" Steve attempted to break down the walls of misconception and misunderstanding which, he believed, on very good evidence, stood in the way of faith in Christ.

Another book "The Truth about Suffering" written with Paul Hansford in 1996, sought to tackle an issue which posed serious questions for Christians and non-Christians alike. Steve was beginning to dip his toe into deep waters. This was even more true in 2003 when his book "The Lost Message of Jesus" raised major theological issues about the Cross and its meaning, causing some controversy in the evangelical world.

The writing of books was a natural extension in the use of the communications skills that Steve had shown as he spoke, week in and week out, up and down the country. His speaking and preaching had been challenging and persuasive from his early days at Tonbridge Baptist Church. Often speaking at length, he had the ability to develop a rapport with his audience and to relate to them and to their lives in a personal way. Basing his addresses firmly on biblical texts or passages, he would use illustrations extensively to emphasise a point, and he would use humour, sometimes against himself, to gain attention and maintain interest. Not infrequently he was deliberately provocative, and like his friend Tony Campolo, was prepared to shock his listeners in order to get them to think independently and 'outside the box'. Similarly, he was not afraid to challenge some interpretations of passages which had hitherto been generally accepted, but which he would argue, were inadequate or wrong. Nor did he shy away from criticising the institutional churches for their failure, as he saw it, to relate to the realities of today's society and for clinging to their liturgies, archaic language, and formal dress codes. Steve was not one to be 'politically correct'. Although he was prepared where necessary to criticise organisations and institutions, he was always sensitive to the needs of individuals, showing understanding and kindness in the face of their predicaments. In his speaking he always sought to empower and envision, to encourage rather than condemn. Above all, his preaching was driven by a passionate desire to bring people into a personal relationship with Jesus Christ and the point where they were willing to give their lives in His service.

It was, however, in the realm of the broadcast media that Steve became best known in the world at large. His exposure on radio and television gave him a public face, which newspapers and journals were

Steve on air, "Where is God? If He is so powerful and so good, why did He allow this to happen?" Her anger was palpable and Steve responded in the best way he could, accepting that people had a right to be angry and to ask God the hard questions that neither he nor any other Christians could answer. Steve accepted later that this TV experience changed his life and that much that he had experienced in TV had shaped his view of the world.

Although Steve was best known as the 'TV vicar' and most of his broadcasting time was devoted to TV, he also contributed frequently on the radio. After his earlier experience with Invicta Radio he contributed over the years to Radio 4's "Sunday" programme and on one occasion preached at a Sunday morning service broadcast from Haddon Hall where Oasis had its offices. A more recent series "Changing Places", presented by Steve on Radio 4, proved to be particularly significant in the development of the Oasis school. The programme took him to Easington, a mining town in the north east of England, seriously depressed by the rundown of the coal industry in the 1980s. In the midst of the social deprivation, Steve visited a school that had recently been built to serve the whole community. He spent two days interviewing local people on how the school had been created and on the contribution that it was making to the redevelopment and renewal of the area. The interviews made a deep impression on him. Following this visit, Steve met officials from the London Borough of Enfield to discuss the possibilities for an Oasis Academy in this area of North London. Drawing on what he had learned in Easington, Steve was able to set out a vision for an Academy which met the approval of the authorities and paved the way for the school described in Chapter 5.

Although Oasis' dealings with the media were largely the result of Steve's own gift as a communicator, he was always encouraging other colleagues to engage with TV, Radio and the Press, and a number did so. Many Christian organisations came to Oasis for help and advice, as they sought to improve their own marketing and publicity. Staff were employed who were skilled in public relations, and the level of activity, including Steve's continuing involvement, was such as to suggest that these activities would be better carried out by a dedicated company, separate from the Trust. Thus, in 1996 the Media Department became a media company or 'Oasis Media' as it was formally known.

The aim of the company was to produce Oasis programmes for use in the media and to provide a service to Charities and other organisations that were not experienced in media work, or perhaps had insufficient media resources of their own. Many charities were doing excellent, high-quality work but were having difficulty in getting this across to the general public and funding agencies. Loll Ingham moved across from GMTV in 1996 to head up the new company and GMTV commissioned Oasis to produce three Oasis Christmas Day shows presented by Steve. Later, the company was commissioned by the BBC to produce a series of programmes for BBC, "Songs of Praise". These featured Cliff (now Sir Cliff) Richard and the work of Tearfund in Bolivia; Gary Linekar and the Great Ormond Street London Children's Hospital, and a transmission from Phoenix, Arizona, USA. The company also produced two series for London Weekend Television (LWT). The first was entitled "Life Hurts" and examined the lives of six young people and their troubled journey through life; the second, "Behind Bars", was concerned with prisoner rehabilitation. In all cases the programmes were designed to be value-based and to have a broad appeal.

Oasis Media advised a number of charities and individuals in their media work. One notable achievement was the winning of the Institute of Public Relations (IPR) award for the work it did on behalf of the charity 'Refuge' to raise the profile of its work on domestic violence.

Over the years Oasis began to discover how to use the complex and challenging world of the media. It did so to the benefit of the Christian Church and of other organizations with similar values. It had also begun to penetrate the secular world with wholesome media values. It is one thing to have something to say but quite another to say it in a way which will ensure that people are listening.

Chapter 11
Establishing Identity

Legal Status

From a strictly legal point of view, the identity of Oasis was established initially in the form of a simple Trust operating under the name "The Ranch Trust", without any stated objects or powers. The initial purpose of the Trust was to provide a legal framework through which Steve's evangelistic ministry could be supported, and funds raised for the proposed new hostel. The name of the Trust had been acquired from others, and in 1986 the Trustees decided to adopt a name of their own. It was therefore changed to "Oasis" in response to Cornelia Chalke's suggestion that this would accurately reflect what she and Steve hoped the hostel would become.

By the early nineties it became clear to the Trustees that in view of the expansion of the Trust's activities and the significant financial risks entailed, a more appropriate legal entity was required. This needed to eliminate the personal risk to Trustees' assets but continue to offer the benefits of full charitable status. Steps were therefore taken in 1992 to convert Oasis into a Company Limited by Guarantee with Charitable Status - the most appropriate legal status for the organisation at its then stage of development. An essential part of this exercise was the need to formalise the Trust's aims and powers in the Company Memorandum, and the operating rules of the Company in the Articles of Association. The new Company began its operations on 1 August 1993. (The formation of the Oasis International Association as a charitable company ten years later was a further step that ensured that cross cultural activities by the independent Oasis organisations throughout the world also fell within an appropriate legal framework.)

The legal framework, important as it was, could not of itself define the essential character or 'soul' of the organisation. Nor could it define how it was perceived by others, or indeed by itself. Like a baby requiring nutrition and love in equal measure, the Trust initially concentrated on acquiring those things necessary to its survival, well-being and growth. With the passing of time, however, it began to develop a self-consciousness and persona that was recognisable and to which others could relate.

Thus, in the early years there was little or no time for introspection or self-analysis. The task of 'introducing people to Jesus' was all consuming, and that of setting up a hostel a formidable challenge which neither Steve nor any of the Trustees had faced before.

Oasis Defined

It was not therefore until the Trust's first Annual Report in 1989, essentially summarising its progress since its inception, that Philip Warland, the Chairman, made an early definition of Oasis as:
- A broad Trust embracing a range of activities
- An enabling Trust committed to training and developing young Christians and,
- A pioneering Trust reflecting the innovative approaches to evangelism for which Oasis was becoming known.

Structures

At around the same time, the Trustees recognised that with the increase in the number of employees to over forty, and with expenditure increasing year-by-year, proper management structures were needed to ensure accountability and efficiency. In discussion with the new leadership team, a three-tier structure was agreed under the governance of the Trustees. This took the form of the leadership team itself, Departmental Heads, each with clearly defined responsibilities, and Project Leaders. Up to that time the Trustees had made a major contribution to the day-to-day management of the Trust, but by 1990 the time had arrived when it was appropriate for the Trustees to revert to a more normal governance role. This change was assisted by the offer of a free external management consultancy by a Christian consultant, Oliver Nyumbu - an offer that was gratefully taken up. Staff were interviewed to identify their gifts, and certain aspects of the organisational structure, including the size and operations of the leadership team, were also examined.

Oasis was becoming less of a club and more of a growing business entity needing appropriate financial, managerial and personnel structures. Annual staff conferences were introduced which brought everyone together, and staff at all levels were asked to discuss 'whole organisation issues' to encourage ownership and cohesion.

Aims

In the early 90's, the Leadership Team began to formalise the principal aims of the Trust. After much discussion involving Department Heads and project leaders, the following aims were agreed.

The aim of the 'Missions Department', at that time renamed 'The Communications Department', was to "communicate the Christian message in a clear and relevant way to people of all ages within and outside the church environment".

The aim of the Trust's 'Training Department' was to "train and motivate Christians of all ages to communicate the Christian message in a clear and relevant way by word of mouth, quality of character and by social action".

Finally, the aim of the 'Social Care Department' was defined as that of "meeting physical, mental, emotional and spiritual needs, especially those of the poor and under-privileged".

The strapline "Introducing people to Jesus" was also re-examined in the light of the wide spread of activities in which the Trust was now engaged. After much heart searching the new caption 'Faith at Work' was agreed.

Values

There remained the challenging task of discovering and expressing the underlying values of the Trust as it sought to understand not just what it did, but how and why it did it. These were published in the 1993 Annual Review, which also contained a re-statement of the Trust's underlying ethos. The agreed values were as follows:-

"We aim to be good news
Oasis exists to show faith at work worldwide, actively to demonstrate the love of God through all we do, say and are - the whole gospel for the whole person.

We get our hands dirty
We preach the good news but we have to earn the right to be heard - our activities must demonstrate our beliefs through healing the sick, feeding the poor and releasing the oppressed. We have to get involved.

We are a team
Individually we have our own God-given gifts and abilities. Together these individual talents form "the body" of Oasis. No member of staff therefore is more important than the next. Each person has a role to play in the vision and direction of the Trust and will be encouraged to take positions of responsibility and accountability.

We believe in equal opportunities
We are actively opposed to discrimination in society and endeavour to demonstrate this through all our activities, including our employment practices.

We strive for excellence
We believe in hard work, commitment and honesty. Whatever we do, we do it to the best of our ability. Budgets may be limited, time may be short, resources may be stretched, but we pursue excellence and the responsible use of resources.

We believe in good ideas
Ideas are our lifeblood. Good ideas are no respecter of persons - we encourage creative thinking and problem solving throughout Oasis. Oasis is all about exploring new possibilities, discovering hidden potential and finding creative, relevant ways of communicating the Christian faith. In this task we encourage effective use of the media.

We are all learners

We believe in the value of training and are committed to developing, equipping and motivating individuals and churches by all appropriate means.

We are pioneers

We are committed to finding new, relevant ways to express eternal, unchanging truths. Whilst we learn from others we will travel our own distinctive path.

We are servants

Our goal is to serve both church and community. Other Christian organisations or denominations are not competitors but partners. We recognise the primary role of the local church.

We depend on God

We rely on God for the provision of money for our work. We have a duty therefore to exercise wisdom and responsibility in its use. The only resources we have are the people who work for us and the God who sustains us. In all things we trust in God, for all that Oasis is and has depends on Him."

These values were revisited in 1996 and a mission statement agreed. It was decided to place the emphasis on God at the beginning to underline the transcendent and fundamental nature of the statement, **"We depend on God.** In all things we trust in God for all that Oasis is and has depends on Him. We have a duty therefore to exercise wisdom and responsibility in the use of all the resources He provides."

As for the mission statement, this was revised to "Oasis aims to demonstrate the Christian faith worldwide through actions as well as words and to equip others to do the same".

Beliefs

By 1990 people were beginning to understand how Oasis saw itself and what it did, but no one had set out what it believed. The leadership had considered the question from time to time but had concluded that time was too short to allow effort to be devoted to theological debate.

137

Instead, the Trustees and the Leadership team decided to adopt the Statement of Faith belonging to the Evangelical Alliance. (Later, at the international level, the International Council adopted the Lausanne Covenant as a way of expressing its solidarity with the worldwide missionary movement).

By the mid 1990s, Oasis knew, or thought it knew, what it was all about and why it existed as an organisation. Certain further refinements were made at the edges, and the underlying concepts expressed in different ways, but generally the die was cast.

There was, however, an emerging issue as to the extent to which Oasis organisations overseas - principally in India - should conform to the same underlying principles. Andy Matheson, now based in Bombay, suggested that the main focus of all Oasis work overseas should be an extension of what had emerged in the UK, but more clearly defined. This was agreed in 1994. Oasis would demonstrate 'faith at work' through holistic ministries, principally to poor and marginalized children and young people in urban areas; it would work through local churches and seek to demonstrate the worldwide nature of the Church through cross cultural ministries. It was accepted, however, that each independent country would be free to apply these principles in ways which were appropriate to the countries concerned. (See chapter 9)

External Symbols

In addition to these introspections, the Trust needed to consider how it was seen by the outside world. Although Steve was becoming increasingly known in the Christian world, the Trustees felt in 1992 that Oasis would be strengthened by the appointment of a Patron(s) and a Council of Reference. The former, ideally a well known person, would provide a figurehead and would be someone to whom the outside world could relate; the latter would assist the Trust by offering advice either individually or collectively, and providing credibility to its work. Clearly, in both cases, the persons appointed needed to be fully in sympathy with Oasis and supportive of all it was trying to do.

Patron

After sounding out a number of names, including the then Archbishop of Canterbury, Lord Tonypandy was appointed as one of the Trust's first patrons. As Speaker of the House of Commons, George Thomas, as he was previously known, was a man of outstanding Christian character, well known for his social concern. Brought up in the Welsh mining valleys, he had seen poverty at its starkest and had risen to high office through the Labour Party. As a Christian and a politician, George Thomas fitted in well with the Trust's holistic agenda. The other patron was Roy Castle. Roy was well known as a committed Christian in the world of entertainment and did much to assist Steve to make his way in the media. He was an outstanding role model for young Christians seeking to witness to their faith in an often sceptical environment. Sadly, Roy died in September 1994 and Steve was asked to speak at his memorial service. All Souls Langham Place was filled with the "great and the good" of the entertainment and broadcasting world, and the service was a great witness to the hope and joy which Roy found in the Christian faith. Following her husband's death, Fiona became a Patron and has since worked tirelessly in support of the Trust. Lord Tonypandy died in 1999 and was replaced by Diane Louise Jordan, well known as a TV presenter and personality. Diane also gave herself unstintingly in support of the work, with a special emphasis on Oasis projects around the world.

Council of Reference

The Trustees decided to appoint twelve people representing a wide range of interests and Christian affiliations, including representatives of the minority ethnic communities. It was agreed that those appointed should ideally be known both outside and within their own denominations. Over a period of about six months, a number of people were approached and a lunch was given in 1993 for those who accepted the invitation. The Council initially consisted of David Coffey, Gerald Coates, Lyndon Bowring, R T Kendall, Clive Calver, Elaine Storkey, Simon Hughes MP (Liberal Democrat), Jeremy Cooke QC, Andrew Wingfield Digby, and Tony Campolo from the USA. Later these were joined by Joel Edwards and two MPs, Andy Reed (Labour) and Gary

Streeter (Conservative). In practice Oasis rarely consulted these people collectively, but each one in different ways and at different times contributed to its life and ministry.

Chapter 12
Working with Others

A Baptist organisation?

Steve, who committed his life to Christ whilst attending a Baptist Church, had studied at a Baptist theological college, and become an ordained Baptist minister. In this sense he was a Baptist through and through, certainly in the early days of his ministry. It is hardly surprising therefore, that as it struggled to establish itself, Oasis was seen by the Christian world as essentially a Baptist organisation.

The close relationship between the denomination and the Trust was also demonstrated by Steve's membership on the Council of the Baptist Union and his nomination for the role of Vice President in 1991 - an appointment which would have led, had he been elected, to the Presidency in the following year.

At the project level, links with Spurgeon's College were also strong, with two of the Trust's innovative courses being run in partnership with the College. These links were recognised by Steve's membership of the College Council and invitations to speak at College speech days and events.

Other projects such as Capital Radiate, and Frontline Teams in Birmingham and the North West, had strong Baptist roots and financial support; and most of the Trust's early missions were conducted in Baptist churches. Oasis also promoted the Action Teams run by the Baptist Missionary Society referred to in Chapter 8.

Without the support and encouragement of the Baptist Union, senior members of the denomination, and Baptist churches at the grass roots, and without financial help of various kinds - project grants, loans, guarantees etc - Oasis might not have survived, let alone grown, in those crucial early phases of its life.

Despite, however, the warmth of these relationships, Oasis did not always see eye to eye with the Baptist 'establishment'. Perhaps this was inevitable. Oasis was a young and innovative organisation with an energetic and visionary leader. Baptist organisations were more conservative, essentially cautious, and deeply set in long but honourable traditions. There was at times a genuine clash of cultures. Steve himself did not always help matters, sometimes raising eyebrows as he made provocative statements designed to challenge people to think more deeply about their faith and effectiveness in the world. His early employment of a driver for his car and his enthusiasm for the then new technologies, especially the mobile phone, marked him out and sent signals that were easily misunderstood by his colleagues in the ministry.

Particular suspicions were raised in the denomination when Oasis appeared to some to 'take over' Haddon Hall Baptist Church in Bermondsey, South London, and a little later, Amott Road Baptist Church in Peckham. Was Oasis setting up a new denomination? Was this the start of a new movement that would attract away the dwindling number of young people attending Baptist churches? In fact, such a plan was not at any time any part of the Oasis strategy, which was firmly focused on Steve's original vision and the imperative to 'introduce people to Jesus'.

Wider Associations

After the first few years Oasis did not, however, see itself as exclusively a Baptist organisation. Those working for the Trust came from a wide range of churches with various denominational allegiances. These were either not known within the office or, if they were, never became an issue. It is not surprising therefore, that with the growth of

Frontline Teams and Steve's extensive preaching programme, church-es from other denominations, ranging from Anglicans to the Brethren and the Salvation Army, would become involved in the life of the Trust. Indeed, two major projects, Christmas Unwrapped and Christmas Cracker, were deliberately designed to reach across denom-inations, paving the way for others such as On Fire, Fanfare and ulti-mately Faithworks.

All these projects sought to bring churches together across towns and cities, embracing churches large and small and giving an impetus to stronger inter-church relationships. The larger projects required joint steering or management committees at local and national levels, the latter usually involving senior figures within the denominations. These projects were immensely encouraging to those who were hop-ing and praying for a unified witness to the outside world, and who saw denominational structures as a hindrance rather than a help to the effective proclamation of the gospel.

There were, nonetheless, costs to the collaboration. On the one hand, where decisions were made by church leaders, it took time to get everyone 'on board' and to secure the involvement of people at the grass roots; on the other, where there were ideas and decisions coming from the grass roots, leaders had to be convinced. Inevitably there was bureaucracy to be avoided or overcome as the different denomination-al structures employed their time-honoured procedures to reach deci-sions. This was, however, a price worth paying as churches realised that they were not isolated islands but part of the national and world-wide church.

Outside the denominational structure Oasis worked closely with the Bible Society and a wide range of other organisations. Some para-church and mission organisations were natural partners, such as YFC, YWAM and OM. Close links were established with Tear Fund and, to a lesser degree, World Vision. Partnerships were formed with Interserve and Latin Link. All these were sustained by personal friend-ship and the shared aim of bringing the Christian message to young people in the UK and abroad. The project Fired Up was a particular tribute to inter-organisational youth work with at least 18 organisations involved.

There were also close relationships with Spring Harvest, New Wine, Soul Survivor and similar organisations. Co-operation with

Spring Harvest was particularly close. Each year, Oasis virtually closed down for several weeks as staff emigrated to the conference sites to provide technical and administrative support, and run children's and youth events. Initially, Steve had a wide range of practical responsibilities, before being asked to speak at seminars and then, in due course, the Big Top. He also sat on the Spring Harvest Council. Oasis was supported financially from time to time from the offering, and its projects given publicity. It did not, however, become an official sponsoring organisation.

Over the years, Steve received invitations to speak from all manner of organisations both in the UK and abroad. He was always reluctant to turn invitations down, until such time as the burdens became intolerable and the cost to Oasis itself too great. Individual organisations and churches sometimes assumed that Steve and Oasis were a 'free good', which they could call upon at a moment's notice. Steps had to be taken, reluctantly, to ration Steve's time and even to charge for his services. This sometimes led to misunderstanding and to a measure of ill feeling on the part of those affected. Regrettable as it was, the Leadership felt that some rationing of the calls on Steve's time was unavoidable.

Government and Statutory Organisations

Relationships between Oasis and secular authorities and organisations became increasingly important as the Trust continued to grow. In the 1980s, many local authorities in inner city areas were hostile to Christian organisations and requests for funds from 'faith based' organisations were often made to an essentially hostile audience, despite the good work to which the money would be put. Progress was, however, made in gaining the respect of the relevant authorities as they recognised the efficient and sensitive management of No3 and the Elizabeth Baxter Health Centre. In the case of the latter, the enthusiastic support of the Health Authority did much to stimulate giving from private trusts and foundations.

At the Central Government level, the hostility was less intense; there was more a sense of suspicion and a reluctance to engage with organisations that might proselytise those of other faiths. The discussion with Central Government about the possibility of an Overseas

From left to right: Sarah Golding, Sarah Mackrill, Andy Matherson, John Nonhebel in first Oasis office in Bombay

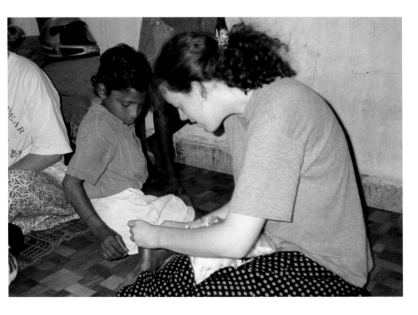

Frontliner dressing a wound in home for street boys, Bombay

Purnata Bhaven or 'House of Wholeness', Igatpuri, near Mumbai, India

1st birthday party at Purnata Bhaven

Stuart Christine briefing Frontline Team in São Paulo, Brazil

Little girl working on rubbish dump in Brazil

Football in Brazilian Favela

Gaining confidence in Harare, Zimbabwe

Skills training in Harare, Zimbabwe

Diane-Louise Jordan in Uganda

Oasis' International Council at Spurgeon's College, London, 2002

not necessarily more acute, than those faced by Charities who make no particular claim to be 'Christian'.

Incoming Resources

In the early days, most of the Trust's income was donated by the friends and supporters of Steve and Cornelia, and of course, by the Trustees. As Steve's work developed, income came in the form of fees from missions, speaking engagements, and, for a time, from the Baptist Union. However, as the Trust expanded its work and took on more paid staff and volunteers, (all of whom still had expenses to be paid), it quickly became clear that a wider base of donors was required and that help would need to be sought from sympathetic Christian Trusts and, where appropriate, other sources of funds. The key decision was also taken in 1990 to develop fee-paying activities, such as training, to provide a sounder long-term financial base.

There were four principal sources of funds, apart from fee income, namely individual supporters, churches, trusts and statutory funding bodies. Companies also provided a potential source of funds but most preferred to assist through the provision of gifts in kind - furniture, computers, food etc.

The need for structures to provide an increasing level of contributions from all sources was easier to understand than it was to implement. It would cost money to employ a dedicated fundraiser and fundraising itself involved other costs, such as publicity, which Oasis could ill afford. Equally Oasis could not afford to continue without a fundraiser if it was to expand its work. The first person to fulfil this role was Jon Brewster who had spent a year on Frontline and who years later became a Trustee. After Jon left, Paul Turner, a recent Maths graduate whose parents were missionaries in Peru, replaced him. Paul began the arduous task of raising funds and building up a supporter base. Slowly and systematically he began to create a database and to manage the annual Gift Day which, coupled with the public celebration event, became one of the most important income generating events of the year. Computer resources were very limited, so each year the exercise involved an enormous effort, drawing in most of the office staff to deal with envelope stuffing and addressing. This increased the sense of teamwork which became very strong in those early days, but diverted resources from frontline activities.

Some of the problems were totally unexpected. For instance, at one stage, Oasis had great difficulty in getting the message across to individuals and churches alike that the Trust's financial position was, more often than not, extremely tight and sometimes precarious. Churches and supporters observed the growth in projects and activities, and with Steve appearing increasingly in the media, the Trust was perceived by some as a flourishing organisation living off the substantial fees which, so it was believed, were received for Steve's services. Nothing could have been further from the truth. Many of Steve's TV commitments were loss leaders designed to give Steve visibility and to establish him in the media, and the fees and expenses received were sometimes insufficient to cover the costs involved.

The fact that Steve possessed one of the early mobile phones, which in the early nineties was seen as a luxury, perpetuated the myth. The phone, which was far too large to carry discretely in the pocket, provided a further reason to some donors to place Oasis low down on their list of funding priorities!

In 1994 Oasis heard through the Evangelical Alliance that a US Charity was in the country exploring ways in which it could help UK charities by providing large grants and assistance with their fundraising programmes. A Christian, John G Bennett, had founded the charity, named New Era Philanthropy, and Oasis immediately took steps to make contact and submit a funding application. After a period of time New Era invited Oasis to a fundraising conference for UK Charities, run in conjunction with the Templeton Foundation. The conference, a relatively lavish occasion at Church House Westminster, was addressed by the Founder and gave opportunity to Oasis staff to build up their relationship with New Era staff. In one of these discussions the Executive Director learnt that NEP were looking for a charity which was prepared to experiment in a UK context, with fundraising methods proven in the United States. For this, NEP would provide guidance, support and new, state-of-the art computer equipment. To the Oasis Leadership this seemed a risk worth taking, and rather than look a gift horse in the mouth they agreed to offer Oasis as a pilot project, an offer gratefully accepted. The result of the new approach increased the proceeds of the Gift Day appeal by nearly 10% and provided technology for fundraising which was to last several years. Sadly, however the enterprise ended in tears. New Era Philanthropy collapsed without warning. Recipients of significant grants in the USA and in the UK were required to return grant monies to enable creditors to be paid, and the Founder received a substantial sentence. The Oasis leadership was thankful that it had not received any money beyond that provided for the fundraising initiative. In due course, despite the circumstances associated with the fundraising grant, Oasis also had to settle with the US Court. Not to do so would have involved disproportionate expense. Many other charities fared far worse.

Young charities face particular problems in their early days, and Oasis was no exception. Whilst they have the advantage of being new, with new ideas and initiatives to excite donors and interest grant making trusts, they have no endowments, no reserves, no track record, and, perhaps equally important, no expectation of legacy income from older people. In this they stand in contrast to many long established charities for whom legacies or the expectations of legacy income, have become an accepted feature of their annual accounts. In the case of Oasis it was rather worse than this. Steve, being a young evangelist with a particular ministry to young people, was increasingly known to thousands of young people throughout the UK. However most of these supporters, being either at school or at college, were not in a position to give significant financial support. (But see Chapter 7 on Christmas Cracker, which shows that it is possible for young people to mobilise financial resources even if they cannot give themselves).

One of the main reasons why a strong supporter base was required was to help to pay for the administrative costs associated with the Trust's activities. For the most part the public is not excited by these costs, preferring instead to give to frontline activities like housing the homeless or providing medical care for AIDS victims. Administrative costs are, however, unavoidable if frontline services are to be provided, but they must also be kept to a minimum if the confidence of donors is to be maintained.

Contributions from grant-making Trusts became increasingly important as the number of projects increased. Oasis' first major social care project, the acquisition of No 3 Cerise Road, was made possible through the generosity of a private donor, the support of the Baptist Union Corporation, and grants from supportive Trusts. The second major social care project, the Elizabeth Baxter Health Centre, was also financed substantially from grants made by a consortium of large donors brought together by the Peabody Trust. Many other capital and recurrent grants were raised over the years and these had the advantage of incorporating sums to meet administrative costs.

Trust fundraising was never easy, requiring specialist skills to be effective. It was also very competitive. Organisations without a track record of success had to convince their prospective benefactors that the money would be spent efficiently on the purposes for which the grants had been made. All new projects understandably required a project proposal and a business plan. Assumptions had to be made about how much of the required cost could be raised from the various bodies to be approached. Without such work no organisation could expect to raise the necessary funds. Many trusts require a project to be up and running, or at least to be assured that the necessary funds for completion will be forthcoming. There is thus a chicken and egg situation. Without finance there can be no project, but without a project enjoying some financial security, money is hard to come by. It is in this situation that the support of major funding bodies, and particularly statutory authorities, can be of vital importance. In both the above projects, support was canvassed and obtained from a wide range of statutory authorities and others with related interests.

Approaches to statutory bodies for grants for social care projects also presented problems because some believed that Oasis would be using the money to proselytise, rather than provide services unconditionally. Oasis never disguised its Christian allegiance and always pointed out that in its social care work it was seeking to carry out Christ's command to love people unconditionally and without any obligation on clients to become Christians in return for the care received -something which was both theologically and practically impossible.

The policy of trying to finance the organisation through fees, though superficially attractive, also had its difficulties. Oasis in its early days was essentially an evangelistic organisation with a strong emphasis on mission throughout the UK. This cost large sums of money for transport and overnight accommodation alone. Initially, Oasis underestimated these costs by a significant margin and the fees charged to churches were much lower than they ought to have been.

152

Chapter 14
Looking to the Future

Oasis is now approaching its 21st birthday. One test of any organisation's strength and vitality is its ability to generate and adjust to further change after years of rapid growth. Some organisations believe that a period of stability is needed once this first phase is passed. Oasis UK itself had to sell the 'move-on' house in Montrell Road, and change the use of the Elizabeth Baxter Health Centre in the face of changing circumstances and financial pressures. This was a serious setback to its social care programme brought about mainly by its failure to obtain statutory funding. But, more generally, Oasis believed that mere consolidation would risk stagnation and ultimately decline. Much of what is described in the earlier pages of this book has provided the launching pad for further developments as Oasis drew on the experience it had gained, and sought new ways of bringing the Gospel to a troubled and unjust world.

In the words of Steve Chalke, the task of the church across the world is "to reflect God and in doing so to demonstrate a faith that works". This aim continued to dominate the thinking of Oasis as it moved into the 21st century. It also inspired the organisation to make plans for the future as set out below.

The Oasis Global family

Oasis is now fully functional in five countries, and operational to one degree or another in a further four, the latest being South Africa.

All are committed to praying and working together; to showing faith at work in a world of need; and to bringing the Gospel in all its fullness to people who are the poor and oppressed, particularly women, children and young people in the great cities of the world. Within this common bond each organisation is working to bring about those changes that are most appropriate to the country concerned, and to do so in culturally sensitive ways. Each is accountable to all the others through the Covenant that they have freely entered into. Key elements will continue to be the training and development of indigenous workers in project management and leadership, and initiatives addressing issues such as human trafficking, (see below), which are common to all. Others include helping those infected and affected by the HIV/AIDS epidemic, particularly in Africa, the welfare of children at risk across the world, and vocational training for young people to enable them to earn a living and the self respect which that brings.

God willing, by 2010 there will be Oasis entities registered in twelve countries drawn together in one family, committed to playing their part in bringing in the Kingdom of God. That is the aim. Oasis envisages a global organisation that is well connected; which shares its resources across the world; which thinks, plans, and prays together strategically: and which aims for the best professionally whilst growing in intimacy with Jesus.[1] Oasis hopes and prays that it can continue to learn from others and share its experience with all those who identify with its aims.

Education

One main strand dominating the future landscape is the continuing need to address fundamental weaknesses and inequalities in school education. Across the world, Oasis has concentrated on the provision of pre-school and primary education because this is seen as the best way of securing a future for children living in poverty by enabling them to access secondary education. Very recently five new pre-schools have been set up in Zimbabwe, now a full member of the

---

[1] Intimacy and Involvement by Steve Chalke and Simon Johnston - published by Kingsway

is also hoped that Oasis will develop other medical and health facilities, including a community hospital. Indeed, as this book goes to press, a new member of staff (Director of Health Development) has been appointed with the remit of engaging with the Department of Health in order to deliver this.

These issues will form an on-going agenda for Oasis throughout the world in the coming years.

A Common Theme and a Major Challenge

The common theme running through all existing programmes, and those which are planned, is the search for a truly holistic approach to the human predicament wherever it is found throughout the world. Every project, whether it is an AIDS orphanage in Africa, helping women to leave prostitution in India, or offsetting educational disadvantage in the UK, is designed to bring about the changes which are necessary to enable poor and vulnerable people to find security and fulfillment in life and, where possible, to facilitate the development of social and economic systems which are just and non-exploitative.

The programmes are all driven by the unwavering belief that God is a God of love and justice, experienced and expressed by individual people and worked out through the Church in the community of the world. They are based on the belief that God hates injustice wherever it is found, and has a particular heart for the poor and oppressed as proclaimed by the Prophets and Jesus himself, as recorded in Luke 4 verses 18 and 19: "*The Spirit of the Lord is on me because He has appointed me to preach good news to the poor. He has sent me to proclaim freedom for the prisoners and recovery of sight for the blind, to release the oppressed, to proclaim the year of the Lord's favour*".

If, however, the work of Oasis and other likeminded organisations is to bring about the Christ-centered transformation of society, it can only happen through the transformation of inner lives of individual people through the work of the Holy Spirit. In other words, external transformation and change can only come through inner transformation and change. Thus, if churches, schools, hospitals and other institutions are to be set up and to pervade society with the values of Jesus Christ, this can only happen if the individuals who are part of those institutions live by and demonstrate to the world the values which He

167

espoused and which, in many cases, are at variance with the values of secular society. Christians will need to show attitudes of love, peace and grace uniquely shown by Jesus during His life and supremely at the cross, where He showed that love is the greatest force in the universe, and forgiveness the greatest healer. Christians following the way of Christ will need to show this unique love for their fellow human beings. For some this may bring "*the favour of all the people*", Acts 2 verse 47 as in the days of the early church, but for others it will bring hostility, abuse, humiliation or disdain.

The characteristics of Christ will be evident in the love of Christians for God's created world and in their efforts to care for it. Christians will be in the forefront of those who seek to save the environment from its present perilous course.

Christians will also need to make changes in their economic behaviour and the way they conduct their working, social and sporting lives, using the Sermon on the Mount in all its aspects, as their template.

Above all, to make all this happen, they will need to be people who are prepared to seek out and understand God, are committed to His purposes, and submitted to the Holy Spirit.

The big question is how can this happen in today's chaotic world of intense pressure brought about by the constant search for personal success and instant gratification, fed by the internet, an intrusive media, the cult of celebrity and the lure of materialism? How can Christians learn to have a living, intimate, relationship with Jesus in all the hubbub and with all the pressure of today's world? And how can believers learn to love God and their neighbour as they leave their comfort zones and open themselves up to their friends and communities? Perhaps these questions should also be on the Oasis agenda in the years that lie ahead.

Conclusion

In 2006 Oasis may have come of age, but it will still seek to move forward under the help and guidance of God. David Livingstone, the great Scottish medical missionary and explorer, is reported to have said, "I will go anywhere provided it is forward". In faith, despite all the challenges, Oasis will seek to do the same.

efforts. Establishing the principle that no project would be run for more than two years, they looked for something quite different which would still catch the interest and imagination of young people.

At that time, the UK government was introducing major changes designed to facilitate radio broadcasting, overseen by a new Radio Authority. Cracker invited churches to set up radio stations across the country and attract money through advertisements and 'dedications'. Whilst doing so they would inform the local community about the needs of the developing world and the local fundraising projects being run at Christmas time to meet them.

Radio Cracker was also promoted by a Cracker video "More than Words" presented by Steve Chalke on location in South America, and the project was launched by the Rt Hon Linda Chalker, Minister of Oversees Development. The Controller of Radio 1 and the Chief Executive of the new Radio Authority were also present.

In all some 90 radio stations were set up in locations as wide apart as Aberdeen in Scotland, Newtonards in Northern Ireland, Southampton in the south of England and Hull in the east. The stations accounted for more than half of those recently licensed by the authority whose Chief Executive congratulated those taking part on the quality and professionalism of their output.

In promoting the project, the Trustees had taken a considerable risk, but good local management and extensive training and advice from people experienced in broadcasting ensured that the number of broadcast 'faux pas' was happily limited.

Overall the project was seen as a great success raising over £540,000. This money was distributed to some 86 causes in 30 countries of the world. Split in terms of category of need, 58% went to people who were disadvantaged or disabled; 36% went towards health education and economic development; 2% to the UK and the rest was used for monitoring and evaluation.

The outcome was particularly gratifying to the Trustees as the UK was in the depths of a severe depression and no project of this kind had been attempted before. The Prime Minister, Rt Hon John Major wrote, "Christmas represents joy and laughter to many families in the United Kingdom. I hope that the proceeds will help to ensure that there are families in the Third World who may have a happier and brighter New

Year, and send everyone associated with the project my very best wishes for its success."

1992 - Radio Cracker and Crackerterias

Radio Cracker was run for a second time in 1992. The capital cost of transmitters alone justified the second round. Some 83 radio stations transmitted broadcasts over a 3.5-mile radius in the four weeks leading up to Christmas. Sky TV provided a national audio link through the Astra Satellite, offering authoritative news broadcasts and an overnight sustaining service to all the radio stations.

In addition, to widen the project's scope and appeal, youth groups were invited to run 'Crackerterias' - simple cafes offering tea, coffee and light snacks charged on the 'Eat Less, Pay More' principle.

A promotional video 'Ignorance is Bliss' was filmed by Steve Chalke on location in India and the launch was sponsored by British Telecom at the BT tower in London.

As part of the process of monitoring and evaluation, a sample survey of those participating showed that on average there were nine people in each management group, 120 people in each wider operational group, and that 75% of those taking part were under 25.

Exceeding the Trust's success in the previous year, over £650,000 was raised and distributed to 32 countries in Central and South America (17%), Eastern and Central Europe (7%), South and Southeast Asia (37%) and Africa and the Middle East (39%).

The Alternative Christmas

The Trustees felt nonetheless that twelve months was a long time to wait for a further fundraising initiative and they sought a way to raise money for a new emergency relief fund by setting up an initiative in mid-summer as an 'alternative Christmas'. The new project, with the strapline "48 hours to Change the World," attracted over 400 groups. Based on the parable of the talents, each group was given £1 by courtesy of the Midland Bank, which they multiplied creatively to raise over £100,000 for use in Bosnia, Africa and India.

1993 and 1994 - Trade and Aid

The development of Crackerterias in 1992 represented early steps in a new initiative to draw attention to the exploitation and poverty arising from unsatisfactory terms and conditions of employment and adverse trading conditions. At the time, a public debate was taking place over the contribution of trade and aid to economic and social development. It was to this issue that the Trustees next turned their attention. The aim was to run a two-year project which would draw attention to the need for trading arrangements to benefit the developing world, and the importance of offering continuing aid to the poorest of the poor. Cracker was not alone in developing these concepts but sought a distinctive approach by emphasising the need for both trade and aid, rather than the importance of one over the other.

The 1993 Trade and Aid Project involved Crackerterias selling 'fairly traded' tea, coffee and other merchandise - day to day beverages brought from the developing world, the purchase of which under specified conditions would bring direct benefits to local employees.

The project was promoted with a video "Manifesto", filmed in Kenya, and was launched at a reception in the House of Commons attended by MPs and senior officials from countries in the developing world. Christmas Cracker also attracted signatories to the 'Greenwich Resolution', which was presented to the Prime Minister at 10 Downing Street. In this document the signatories resolved, "To stand against apathy, pride and greed, violence and aggression, prejudice and ignorance, and cynicism and unbelief". It included the statements,

"For those who have the means to trade, we will use our power as young Christian consumers in an informed way to work for fair, right and just reward for producers and workers. For others, who are marginalised beyond even the most basic living standards, we will reach out in Christian love and concern to give our aid and plant the seeds of a future hope."

In so acting, Cracker stood alongside other organisations such as the Jubilee Campaign who were putting pressure on the government to relieve the debt of the Developing World.

In all, two hundred groups took part in the Trade and Aid Project, raising £200,000 for disbursement by the Trust. Some £66,000 went to ten countries in Africa; £41,000 to six countries in Central and South

America; £61,000 to six countries in South and South-east Asia and £22,000 to Russia and Romania. The total money raised from all the Trust's activities during this period, reached a peak of £770,000.

The Trade and Aid theme was continued in 1994. Activity was concentrated on 129 "Really Useful Present Stores" and 251 additional fundraising events. These stores were set up throughout the UK to emphasise further the importance of fair trade. Trade turnover to the tune of over £0.25 million was achieved. This produced a trading surplus of £36,000, which together with the proceeds of fundraising events enabled the Trustees to distribute a further £200,000.

1995 and 1996 -The Final Phase - Cracker Newspapers

Following two years of Trade and Aid, the Trustees were at pains to come up with another project to capture the imagination of the young people who had given so much of their time and energy to earlier Cracker endeavours. It seemed that the most promising approach and one that had already proved a great success, was to focus again on the media. The idea of the Cracker Newspaper was subsequently born, supplemented as usual by fundraising events.

The aim of the 1995 project was to draw attention to the many young people at risk from the sex trade, especially young girls involved in forced prostitution, and to raise funds to assist Christian organisations working to free young people from this particularly offensive form of modern slavery. The promotional video was produced in Bangkok.

Participants in the local churches were offered the usual training and support. In all, some 200 individual editions of 'The Cracker' were produced and around £250,000 raised by about 300 groups.

In 1996, the interest and participation of Sightsavers International offered the prospect of a second successful year for the Cracker Newspaper idea. Sightsavers sponsored the project with a substantial sum of money and worked closely with the Cracker team to make the project - designed to fight preventable blindness - a success.

Huge efforts were made to promote the project throughout the UK and special efforts were made to involve schools for whom the production of a newspaper was particularly user friendly.

A video "Blind Truth" on preventable blindness in Bangladesh was presented by Steve Chalke and anchored by Trevor McDonald, the ITV news presenter, who also attended the launch. Boots also donated £1,000 for a "Boots Optician Young Journalist of the Year Award".

As before, the Cracker team provided extensive resources in support of the video, which was sent to all registered groups. Groups also received a registration certificate, a newspaper guide, an events guide, discs with compulsory artwork, national articles, quotes etc., a copy of 'Cracking Up', a 'Cracker' letterhead and ID template, a financial return form, an artwork sheet, a letter of introduction and a merchandise brochure. All church based groups were contacted by direct mail and there was a promotional tour in the summer with extensive advertising in the Christian media.

Despite all these efforts, the outcome was disappointing to both Sightsavers and the Cracker Trustees. In all only 140 groups took part in the UK and 83 newspapers were produced, of which twenty came from schools. There were a mere 57 events.

Although some £150,000 was distributed to twenty projects in eight countries, the project had not lived up to expectations and it was clearly time to assess whether Christmas Cracker had run its course.

The 'Cracker' Projects
Summary Table

Year	Project	Nº of Local Projects	Money Distribution (£'s)
1989	Cracker Restaurants	226 'Eat-less-pay-more' Restaurants	406,827
1990	Cracker Restaurants	520 Events	522,619
1991	Radio Cracker	80 Events 90 Radio Stations	541,325
1992	Radio Cracker Alternative Christmas	280 Crackerterias 83 Radio Stations 400 Groups registered	669,849 100,000
1993	Trade & Aid Fired Up/Streets Apart GMTV Projects	200 groups 530 groups TV Appeal	196,150 59,000 517,000
1994	Trade & Aid Fired Up GMTV Carol Concert	129 Really Useful Present Stores 251 Events	156,000 17,330 10,483
1995	Cracker Newspapers	200 Editions 300 Groups	250,000
1996	Cracker Newspapers	140 Groups 83 Editions 57 Events	150,000
	International Cracker	Australia, New Zealand, Switzerland, Netherlands, South Africa & USA	160,000

Appendix C
Oasis International Council

Covenant

Preamble

Following the meeting of the Oasis International Council in São Paulo on 13 and 14 September 2000, we, the signatories to this document, enter into the Covenant set out below.

Terminology

Oasis UK means the Oasis Charitable Trust, incorporated as a Company Limited by Guarantee on 18 may 1993.

Oasis India means a Social Service Organisation, registered under the Karnataka Societies Registration Act India (Nr S 690 - 94/95) in 1994.

Oasis Brazil means the Associação Batista de Incentivo e Apoio ao Homem, registered with the Municipal District of São Paulo, Brazil, as a charitable entity of a social and educational nature, on 10 May 1990.

International Council means the body set up by the parties having the functions and powers set out in the Covenant.

International Office means an office, set up by the Council, with the functions and powers set out in the Covenant, and with a Director who has been appointed to execute the Council's decisions.

Limits:

Notwithstanding any other provisions contained in this Covenant, no action taken by the Oasis International Council shall have the effect, or be deemed to have the effect, of infringing in any way upon the autonomy of any national body to the extent that the legal and charitable status of such national body shall be jeopardised in any way by any such action.

Article 1
Constitution

1.1 <u>Form</u>

We, having a common vision, mission and statement of faith, hereby covenant to co-operate in the conduct of our ministries.

1.2 <u>Name</u>

We will co-operate through a Council and Office operating under the name Oasis International.

1.3 <u>Purpose</u>

The purpose for which Oasis International is organised shall be to undertake and facilitate work in accordance with the objects, powers and authority of Oasis UK, Oasis India and Oasis Brazil, and such other organisations authorised to bear the name Oasis.

1.4 International Office

The office shall be located initially in the United Kingdom, but may in due course be located in such other places as we, the parties to this agreement may from time to time designate.

Article 2
Areas of Co-operation

As legally independent organisations bearing the name Oasis, we commit ourselves to

- pray for and encourage one another in our national and international ministries
- co-operate with one another in cross-cultural matters
- support and help one another according to need and ability
- agree policies and guidelines relating to cross-cultural ministry

-   communicate and consult with one another and agree all those ministries of our respective organisations which are conducted outside our individual national boundaries.

Article 3
Organisation

3.1 <u>The International Council</u>
The Council shall be comprised of the following members:
-   The Chairperson of each national body party to this agreement.
-   The Chief Executive (or equivalent) of each national body party to this agreement.
-   Steve Chalke as the Founding President (ex officio).
-   A Chairperson (hereafter referred to as 'The Chairperson of the International Council'), appointed by the Council.
-   An International Director appointed by the Council, who shall be the Secretary of the Council.

Each national body shall have the right to appoint an alternative person to attend and to vote at any meeting of the Council, in place of its Chairperson/Chief Executive.

The International Council, which will be convened by the Chairperson of the Council, will normally meet at least once every two years or at such other times or frequency as he/she may decide in consultation with the International Director, President and national bodies.

3.2 <u>Voting</u>
Each national organisation represented on the Council shall have two votes. In the event of a tie the Chairperson of the Council will have the casting vote.

3.3 <u>Co-options</u>
The Council shall have the power to co-opt members for particular meetings; co-opted members may speak but are not permitted to vote.

Article 4
Functions and Powers

The functions of the Council shall be as follows:

4.1 To approve the Statements of Faith, Mission and Vision and the Policy Guidelines.

4.2 To promote Oasis internationally and to maintain its unity and integrity throughout the world.

4.3 To co-ordinate the work of Oasis internationally and strengthen relationships between its members.

4.4 To provide information and advisory services as needed.

4.5 To oversee and approve the strategic development of Oasis internationally.

4.6 To agree on the formation and participation of additional national bodies who desire to bear the name Oasis, and the criteria governing such participation (see Article 9)

4.7 To decide on those policy issues which are, by agreement of the national bodies, reserved to the Council.

4.8 To agree all matters of policy in relation to trans-national issues and to provide guidelines.

4.9 To sanction any national body which breaches this Covenant or which in any way brings the name of Oasis into disrepute (see Article 6).

4.10 To represent Oasis, together with member bodies as appropriate, in its relations with other worldwide organisations.

4.11 To delegate, at its discretion, any of its functions and powers to the International Director.

Article 5
Finance

5.1 The Council shall prepare a budget for each year and recommend the approved amount to each national body.

5.2 The approved expenditure of the Council, including its officers, shall be borne by allocation from the funds of the respective national bodies, supplemented by direct gifts and any earning of its officers.

5.3 The Council shall keep an account or accounts at such bank or banks as it shall from time to time determine, and cheques shall be drawn, signed and endorsed by such person or persons as the Council shall from time to time direct.

5.4 The Council shall keep full and proper accounts as required by law. Such accounts shall be audited once per year by auditors appointed by the Council.

Article 6
Terms and Termination of Membership

Oasis International shall continue until terminated by agreement between its member bodies. Any member body may terminate its participation in this agreement by giving written notice, with reasons, to the Council, such termination to become effective one year from the date of the notice or at such other time as the parties shall mutually agree.

The council shall have powers to terminate after six months notice, or if circumstances justify it without notice, the participation in Oasis International of any national body, whose policies, principles or practices, in the opinion of the Council, do not conform to those contained in this Covenant.

Any national body, which is no longer part of Oasis International, will no longer have the right to attend Council meetings or use the Oasis branding. The Council will have the right to state publicly the reason(s) for the termination of membership.

Article 7
Minutes

Minutes of Council meetings shall be prepared and approved by the Chairperson of the Council, within 21 days of the last day of each meeting, and circulated to Council members within 30 days of the said meeting.

Article 8
Amendments

Amendments to this Covenant may only be made following two months written notice and at a properly convened meeting of the Council. Before final incorporation of amendments in the Covenant, national bodies will be asked for their final assent to the amendment(s) concerned.

Article 9
New Members

Any organisation having the same mission and vision as the parties to this Covenant, sharing the same statement of faith, subscribing to the Lausanne Covenant and wishing to use the name Oasis, may become a party to this Covenant and a member, on its execution, of Oasis International, subject to the written consent of all the parties. On the Execution of this Covenant, such an additional party shall be bound by all the provisions of the Covenant from the date thereof.

Article 10
Integrity of the Name 'Oasis'

In seeking to be one interdependent global entity made up of legally registered bodies in countries where we work, we covenant together to uphold the integrity of the name 'Oasis'. We agree that, where the integrity of that name comes into question in one location, together we shall seek to bring influence into the situation as a corporate body. We further agree that, where the Council speaks to us in this regard, we will as Country Boards and Directors treat what is said with due seriousness.

Oasis International
Statement of Faith

Oasis International subscribes to the following Statement of Faith.

- The sovereignty and grace of the triune God, God the Father, God the Son and God the Holy Spirit in creation, providence, revelation, redemption and final judgement.
- The Divine inspiration and infallibility of Scripture as originally given and its consequent entire trustworthiness and authority in all matters of faith and conduct.
- The universal sinfulness and guilt of fallen man, making him subject to God's wrath and condemnation.
- The substitutionary sacrifice of Jesus Christ, the incarnate Son of God, as the sole and all-sufficient ground of redemption from the guilt and power of sin and from its eternal consequences.
- The justification of the sinner solely by the grace of God through faith in Christ who was crucified and bodily raised from the dead.
- The illuminating, regenerating, indwelling and sanctifying work of God the Holy Spirit.
- The priesthood of all believers, who form the universal Church, the Body of which Christ is the Head, and which is committed by His command to the proclamation of the Gospel throughout the world.
- The expectation of the personal, visible return of the Lord Jesus Christ in power and glory.

It also subscribes to the Lausanne Covenant.